PRAISE FOR *THE TAO OF INFLUENCE*

"Some twenty years ago, a quote came across my desk that has been with me ever since: 'Who you are speaks so loudly that no one will ever hear a word you're saying.' Karen McGregor's *The Tao of Influence* expands on that concept, bringing to our awareness just how our State of Consciousness informs our thoughts, words, and ultimately our deeds. A book that is both spiritual and oriented towards happiness and success is what I am always looking for. In that search, *The Tao of Influence* is an exquisite find! Read these pages, feel the Tao, get into the Holy Flow and Have the Best Day Ever!"

—David "Avocado" Wolfe, nutritionist, author, adventurer, health activist, organic/biodynamic farmer, www.davidwolfe.com

"Everyone is on a journey to unravel their true purpose and create the impact and influence they know is possible. I regularly ask God/the Universe, 'Please help me understand your will.' This has often led to being thrown into tough circumstances! While it may not be what we think we want, it helps us learn new perspectives. *The Tao of Influence* does a great job of helping you realize that in the midst of all this, coming from a place of love and compassion in trying times is the key to lasting influence and true leadership."

—Brian Smith, UGG Founder

"This inspiring book is a leadership gem! It merges the ancient wisdom of the Tao with both deep inner growth practices and highly effective outer action steps necessary to create impact and influence in the world. Karen McGregor's unique and insightful process into the heart of true influence will accelerate and escalate your leadership achievement and path."

—Dr. John Demartini, international bestselling author of
The Values Factor

"This is not the typical leadership book. In *The Tao of Influence*, Karen McGregor applies ancient wisdom to the current day challenges we experience in business, in our families, and in our global community… This book offers a path to a higher level of influence and to a richer life for you and for those around you."

—Marci Shimoff, international speaker, cofounder of Your Year of Miracles and *New York Times* bestselling author of *Happy for No Reason, Love for No Reason*, and *Chicken Soup for the Woman's Soul*

"A Knowledge Keeper has great responsibility in sharing what he or she knows. In this beautifully written book, Karen McGregor proves her worth in sharing the teachings of *The Tao Te Ching*. She understands. She is responsible. Karen helps us understand how to use ancient wisdom in our daily lives by creating better relationships with ourselves and the people around us. By translating *The Tao Te Ching* into simple steps for greater influence, Karen has created a powerful tool for today's leaders."

—Andrea Menard, Métis Song Keeper and founder of the Sacred Feminine Learning Lodge

"A must-read book for change agents and difference makers! *The Tao of Influence* is a tribute to Karen McGregor's great wisdom in supporting people to impact the world both in who they are and by what they do. Karen McGregor is a modern-day influencer and an amazing teacher. I've watched her light the spark of self-transformation in thousands. She is a master at helping people see the patterns that keep them from moving forward to a happy, healthy, impactful life."

—Teresa de Grosbois, founder and chair of Evolutionary Business Council and international bestselling author of *Mass Influence*

"The original TAO states that the true Tao can never be spoken. This is true AND The Ancient Ones never met Ms. Karen McGregor, author of *The Tao of Influence*! WOW! For centuries, men have tried to interpret this ancient, orally transmitted masterpiece of wisdom for simplicity and guidance. It's commonly known as 'The Way of Life.' This masterpiece is now interpreted for us by a woman to help us digest its profound wisdom in the twenty-first century. The simple elegance that Karen masterfully teaches us can now influence us living in the modern age.

"She has manifested the wisdom of the inner mystery of the ages to be used outwardly in our everyday lives. No small task. The ancient TAO clearly states that 'the underdog always wins.' Karen has now won her place in human history as one of the first women to update this timeless treasure for us all. What a profound gift. Do you want the whole ball of wax in one book? This is it! Forget therapy, how-to, or any other kind of self-help book out there. It's all in here, end of story. I'm deeply moved to tears. Thank you Karen for caring enough to guide and teach us about the updated Way of Life we so need today."

—Gary Stuart, two-time bestselling author

"Karen McGregor has provided a critical roadmap for today's leaders. She shares with great clarity the steps to merge ancient wisdom practices and philosophies with modern day, hands-on tools to be the leader that positively influences not only by what they do, but more importantly, by who they are being in all of the doing."

—Valerie René Sheppard, multi-award-winning, #1 international bestselling author of *Living Happy to Be ME!*

"In her book, *The Tao of Influence*, Karen McGregor offers us the map to living, serving, and leading powerfully. By integrating ancient principles with the depth of her intuitive wisdom and steps for profound inner growth, we are given the keys to becoming a leader of influence and impact at the highest level. This should be required reading for all thought leaders and change agents or anyone wanting to make a positive difference in the world!"

—Eva Gregory, CPCC, founder of Leading Edge Coaching & Training, mentor to spiritual entrepreneurs worldwide, and author of *The Feel Good Guide to Prosperity* and *Life Lessons for Mastering the Law of Attraction,* coauthored with Jack Canfield

"A must read! The insights in this cutting-edge book are a refreshing take on how we create real impact in the world. Karen McGregor has a beautiful blend of practical steps and esoteric principles that merge to create a new powerful roadmap to support anyone wanting to create positive influence in the world."

—Sandra Yancey, founder and CEO of eWomenNetwork, Inc.

"Power. Purpose. Presence. Potential—all words that speak to the magnificence of the human condition in its highest form. Karen births a masterful work that exposes and shares how all of us may tap these foundational principles to lead a life filled with intention, joy, and results (as any of us may choose to define them.) A must read for all seekers and anyone searching for deeper meaning and truth."

—Ridgely Goldsborough, Buddhist scholar, bestselling author of seventeen books, and founder of www.MindTypes.com

"There is an ancient way of wielding leadership that is ripe for our time—and that is *The Tao of Influence*. Karen McGregor has gifted us with not only ideas, but a deep transmission as to how to move ourselves, our families, and our teams into a struggle-free way of positive change and evolution. She brings the old Tao back in a pragmatic and tender way to replenish our weariness and shift us from force to freedom. Devour this gem and experience greater ease, joy, and fulfillment."

—Satyen Raja, founder of WarriorSage Trainings

"Today, more than ever, the world is yearning for positive influencers. We've observed the fall of corrupt companies, institutions, and leaders. While we have lost faith and belief in them, we have not yet replaced them with positive alternatives. Karen McGregor provides these alternatives in *The Tao of Influence*. This book addresses the deepest yearnings of influencers, including the journey from self-growth to standing for altruistic global needs for change. Her four pillars walk you through the journey to ultimate love. Read it and watch your influence expand to serve the planet."

—Dr. Manon Bolliger, ND and founder of Bowen College

"Karen McGregor has an extraordinary balance of being/doing and creating personal growth systems that work for leaders in times of global upheaval. She has shared her expertise and wisdom at the Global Influence Summit, an event that attracted global influencers and leaders from around the world. Karen's commitment to supporting changemakers and leaders is evident in everything she does, including her latest book, *The Tao of Influence*, where she provides much needed direction and support in this time of global change."

—Charmaine Hammond, MA, CSP, professional speaker and bestselling author

"With traditional systems and structures crumbling all around us, now more than ever we need Karen McGregor's inspired brand of ancient and cutting-edge wisdom that gives thought leaders the tools to promote the principles of living in alignment with our most authentic selves for a more compassionate and sustainable planet. *The Tao of Influence* provides a 'heart map' of sorts: a masterful blend of the personal and the universal that Radiance readers and beyond will benefit from for lifetimes to come."

—Scott Ware, president of Radiance Multidimensional Media & Magazine

"When you mix 'Tao—A Way' with 'Influence—Your Way,' you're bound to experience a natural pathway to live your extraordinary life. From Karen's lived experience she offers four pillars to navigate your journey and its associated destinations. Practical, down to earth, and in plain language, *The Tao of Influence* is worth the read. More so, it's worth your time and effort to use this book as a map to make it happen for you and those you love!"

—Dr. Stephen Hobbs, cofounder of the International Mentoring Community

The Tao of Influence

The Tao of Influence

ANCIENT WISDOM FOR MODERN LEADERS AND ENTREPRENEURS

Karen McGregor

Mango Publishing
CORAL GABLES

For permission requests, please contact the publisher at:
Mango Publishing Group
2850 S Douglas Road, 2nd Floor
Coral Gables, FL 33134 USA
info@mango.bz

For special orders, quantity sales, course adoptions and corporate sales, please
email the publisher at sales@mango.bz. For trade and wholesale sales, please
contact Ingram Publisher Services at customer.service@ingramcontent.com or
+1.800.509.4887.

The Tao of Influence: Ancient Wisdom for Modern Leaders and Entrepreneurs

Library of Congress Cataloging-in-Publication number: 2020933896
ISBN: (print) 978-1-64250-275-6, (ebook) 978-1-64250-276-3
BISAC category code BUS071000, BUSINESS & ECONOMICS / Leadership

Printed in the United States of America

For my mother, my first teacher of love.

Table of Contents

Foreword

The first time I read Lao Tzu's masterpiece, the *Tao Te Ching*, I had recently finished my studies at a respectable Jesuit university in Chicago. Within weeks of graduation, I'd met the woman I would one day marry, and she exposed me to mystical traditions of other religions and philosophies, including the fresh and exciting world of New Age spirituality, which was just beginning to emerge. One of the first things that drew me to Linda was her spiritual curiosity; it was something I could relate to, but only through the perspective of my Catholic upbringing.

Within days of meeting her, I devoured my first non-Catholic spiritual book—Paramahansa Yogananda's *Autobiography of a Yogi*—and my world was forever changed. I began to haunt the shelves of the tiny New Age bookshop around the corner from my apartment. It was filled with crystals, channeled books and tapes, and a wide assortment of other out-of-the-box material that made my mind spin. Everything there was fresh and exciting, and it made me feel like I was part of something important, something that might one day change the world. It was 1984, and my life had found a new orbit.

The next book I read was the *Tao Te Ching*.

How is it possible that such wisdom existed without me knowing about it? It's true: I was a bit sheltered—okay, maybe more than "a bit"—but the book was so far beyond anything I had been exposed to before, that I could almost feel the earth shaking beneath my feet. A gentle presence drifted around me like incense as I read each page.

And that's what brings me to Karen's profound offering.
Presence! That was the key, and that's what Karen captures in this
wonderful new book.

When I agreed to write this foreword, I thought I would have a lot
to say. After all, the *Tao Te Ching* has been a staple in my spiritual
diet since I first discovered it all those years ago. But now, as I sit
writing these words, I find myself nearly mute, as if the words are
less important than the presence they inspire. Isn't that what Lao Tzu
hoped to communicate? How many books have passed through the
centuries with such grace because the author never sought to institute
a religion or even a spiritual community? Lao Tzu simply responded
to the heartfelt request of someone who had benefited from his
wisdom and convinced him to write it down. And we are the grateful
beneficiaries of that request.

Is *The Tao of Influence* about how to embody the Tao to influence
people—or is it about something deeper? The answer to both
questions is: "Yes." The only true influence we have is our presence.
Words alone can never come close to the deep communication
produced by a simple smile or an energetic embrace, especially if we're
not trying to change the other person. And that's the key. Trying to
change someone to meet our idea of who they should be is a misuse of
what Lao Tzu would call the "true Tao." *The Tao of Influence* is about
influence, but not from the level of control or ego. We are called to
inspire people to become "influencers" in a world that's very much
in need of positive examples. When we use our presence in this way,
people—and even the world—can be transformed.

I can certainly attest to this in my own life. I've seen that presence
is the great influencer; concepts are not. For over twenty years,
I've traveled around the world to share peace concerts in troubled
countries like Bosnia, Iraq, and Northern Ireland. As a Peace
Troubadour, I demonstrate the power of presence through song,
and now and then, through a few well-placed words. As St. Francis

of Assisi said: "Our only job is to teach the gospel wherever we go, and, when necessary, use words." Each time I traveled to a country at war to perform the Peace Concert, I would invite people to join their prayerful intentions together at the same time, and extend it to the country I was performing in. Millions of people often responded, not due to any power of my personality, but due to the presence behind my personality—the presence of I AM, which we all share.

Now, something new has come along that is just as powerful as the *Tao Te Ching*. Karen brings into focus something that is so important for the times we find ourselves in. If anything is going to save our world, what she describes here will! It's one thing to watch the world spin out of control—it's quite another to offer the balm that the world needs to heal and transform. This book captures what I'm trying to describe here, and we are all blessed for it.

James Twyman, Peace Troubadour

Ajiic, Mexico

October 23, 2019

Introduction

It was the day of my father's funeral. I woke up in the basement of my parents' home, and slowly walked up the stairs, reflecting on what it meant to no longer have my dad in my life—to never hear his hearty laughter and never see his brilliant smile again. I was only thirty-four, and my dad had been a big influence on my life.

I opened the front door to get some fresh air and noticed a letter tucked under the doormat that was addressed to the Brust family. Hoping to spare my grieving mom from having to read what I suspected was yet another sympathy card, I opened the envelope and found inside it a piece of paper that had been folded several times. The gesture seemed to suggest that the contents were important; that the note shouldn't be ignored or tossed in a pile with similar sentiments.

I carefully unfolded the paper, revealing a handwritten letter from someone I didn't know. I learned from her letter that she was a neighbor who lived directly across the street, and she was almost due to give birth to her second child. The letter began as most sympathy cards do. "I'm terribly sorry for your loss." But then she shared something that stuck with me all these years later.

"I never knew Gunther. We never spoke a word to each other, but I would gaze out my window every day and watch him build a birdhouse or a new piece of furniture in the back yard, putting up a new fence, and fixing things that needed repair. I watched him do these things with a smile on his face, and I thought to myself, 'Wow, I hope that my husband will be the kind of man Gunther is.' He gave me hope and inspired me to have a beautiful home and family too. He changed my life, and he didn't even know it. Now, I want you to know it."

Tears welled up in my eyes, and I couldn't speak as I took the letter to my mom. I had always thought of my dad as a simple man who loved nature, stories, and a good laugh several times a day. But I realized that day, and again later at his celebration of life, that my dad *influenced* people in many ways—some obvious and some not. And so, I was inspired to understand the nature of influence. What causes people to be influential, and why? What traits do people have in common that influence the world for the better?

I knew one thing for sure: I wasn't searching for typical answers found on the internet or in one of the hundreds of books written on the topic. I wasn't interested in antiquated definitions of influence that pit "getting" vs. "giving" or manipulating vs. inspiring. I knew that those who ignite profound change in our world have often acted as sacred messengers of a higher order of influence. Their influence, in fact, is not necessarily neatly packaged; it grows in depth and richness as it is embraced and experienced.

So, my journey had begun; I wanted to explore the mystery of *influence* from all sides and angles. I attended talks with inspirational speakers and received training to become a speaker myself, eventually being guided to train messengers around the world to have more influence. I interviewed accomplished business owners about their influence and success, and then dove into entrepreneurship myself in the field of public speaking and sales training. I studied with spiritual mentors to understand influence from a different angle. Each experience and each conversation led me to observe influence from yet another perspective.

My explorations expanded before me. Any time I started to think that I finally had a handle on what influence was, I would inevitably be guided to new conversations with people who shared with me what influenced them to make lasting changes, and how they influenced others. I witnessed my own impact on my public speaking clients in ways that I could not predict. While I observed, researched, and interviewed, I read everything I could about the finer subtleties of influence, and learned much more. Yet, there was one powerful text that I continued to come back to—a wisdom text that invited me to experience over and over again the nature of true influence: the *Tao Te Ching*.

Influence and the Tao Te Ching

The *Tao Te Ching* is a collection of eighty-one verses written over four thousand years ago by Lao Tzu, a Chinese prophet. He wrote it in response to a desert gatekeeper, Yin Hsi, who begged him to record the profound teachings he had been sharing. Many scholars consider the *Tao Te Ching* one of the wisest books ever written. When applied to influence, the principles of the *Tao Te Ching* shift the fabric of our thinking and behaviors to help create a vibrant world of growth and potential.

Today, more than ever, we find ourselves in a crisis in which many of us are yearning for positive influencers. We are hoping for real, authentic, heart-driven people who can create lasting change on the planet. In less than two decades, we have watched the rise of technology contribute to excess noise, distractions, and a myriad of choices that keep most people unfocused and uncertain as to what to believe. At the same time, we've observed the fall of corrupt companies, institutions, and leaders. While we have lost faith and belief in them, we have not yet replaced them with positive alternatives. We feel a tangible void, and like nature, the vacuum eventually gets filled—one way or another. The question is: with what?

This void puts us at a vulnerable point in history—we can choose to step into it and become a positive influence, or we can allow more and more apathy and darkness to fill it. There is currently a trend of celebrity influencers; while some of them are indeed creating positive change, those are not typically the ones that the masses are paying attention to over the long term. Huge numbers of people are following those who are loud, large, and spiritually bankrupt. They are voting them into public office. The consequences of doing so are now coming to light, but the masses feel they have nowhere else to turn.

Yet, if enough of us turn inwards to our own capacity to create change—real, lasting, evolutionary change on the planet—we can fill the void, and create a new world rooted in love. The *Tao Te Ching's* principles and philosophies support influential thinking and actions that are based in love. This book aims to help you ground the wisdom of the Tao into your everyday reality through practical, daily steps.

As we begin our journey, it's useful to look at the current situation of old-world influencers: the clear majority of whom came from educational, political, and religious environments consisting of traditional schools, churches, and government-led organizations. The majority of these influencers went on to work in those same establishments, where they generated a great deal of good, and upheld strong values. Yet, now we find these institutions crumbling at our feet, the Millennials and Generation Z having no wish to follow in their footsteps. The reason? The type of influence they stood for is not lasting. Young people are saying "no" to patterns of behavior that, although they have become the accepted norm over a long period of time, rarely foster real and powerful change within ourselves and in our world.

Three Stages of Influence

Because most of us have witnessed both the positive and negative results of people's influence over others, let's first examine the development of influence, and how it shows up in our lives. In my research, I've learned that most people go through three stages of influence, and you may notice this progression in yourself. The first stage is self-centered, aligned with the old paradigm of influence, and all about attempting to get something we want. For example, we may have good intentions, such as providing for our young children, qualifying for a first mortgage, or getting that dream job, but the focus is entirely on "me," and what I need and want for my life. Sometimes, manipulation, greed, control, or another fear-based behavior shows up. Consequently, results are minimal, and often don't last beyond the individual's goal.

The second stage of influence happens when the influencer understands that the goal is a "win-win." They want everyone involved in the decision or action to benefit. Influencers at this stage care deeply enough to ensure that everyone feels that their own desire and goal has been met.

The third stage of influence is when the influencer is working toward a powerful outcome for all—for the planet, the community, and the evolution of humanity. This is the Tao at work—selfless contribution, where the leader's invisible strength ignites great change. The *Tao Te Ching* reminds us that the sage "does not claim greatness over anything. He's not even aware of his own greatness." Influencers in this third stage are not concerned about getting something for themselves or about being seen or noticed. They no longer require that their personal needs get met; they're focused on working toward change on the planet. As Satyen Raja, one of my spiritual mentors, shared with me, "The heart of influence is devotion to people's evolution. That's the source of it being the purest, and most powerful."

The Three Stages of Influence

- Self-centeredness
- Win-win Mentality
- Selflessness

The most powerful influencers don't try to be influencers for egoic reasons. They are not struck by the praise or recognition of having an impact. Raw food advocate and superfoods expert David Wolfe, says, "I don't like to be after influence for influence's sake. Influence has to do with our ability to alter the direction that our world is heading. To me, that's a spiritual directive." David says he wants to see the world different than it is now, and as an activist, promotes far less use of chemicals, a vast decrease in artificial synthetic materials going into the environment or being disposed of in the environment, and huge changes in methods of farming and interacting with the earth. David's message and action over the last two decades has transformed many people's choices, and he continues to influence people worldwide to wake up to their personal and collective choices for themselves, and for the earth. He demonstrates the heart of influence: acting for the good of all, and for our planet.

The Four Pillars

While training people over the past decade to share their messages on stage and reach for their full potential, I came to identify four pillars of influence that determine whether lasting, sustainable change occurs. These pillars are: Power, Presence, Purpose, and Potential. Understanding these four pillars from a spiritual and personal perspective and integrating them into our lives allows the principles of the Tao to naturally become part of everyday life. Real and lasting positive change begins to happen. Movements ignite. People awaken. Miracles become the norm. That's why I wrote this book.

Life itself is all about navigating personal power, so the first pillar, Power, delves into your relationship with it. In every choice, in every thought, in every action you make, you either accentuate or diminish your power. And each time you do so, you impact not just yourself, but everyone and everything around you. In this book, we will look at all the places where power has been distorted and bring it back to light. By doing so, you'll see the Butterfly Effect at work: the smallest of choices can set in motion a myriad of consequences. Walking in the Way of the Tao, you'll learn to choose, so that your personal power has the greatest impact. You'll learn to understand and activate the power of your words, your thoughts, and your commitment to that which you wish to change.

The second pillar is Presence, and we will explore your relationship to it. Presence is the ability to exist in the moment with no thought of past or future. All great spiritual teachers have noted that the key to fulfillment and joy is to learn to be in the now. It is also critical to developing influence, since people who are present and in the fullness of life as it exists here and now are the same people who are fully trusted, counted on for their wisdom, and able to move mountains with their words. Gandhi, Jesus, and Mother Theresa were all examples of people who shifted the course of history and taught great things with their presence and power. As Gandhi said, "Be the change you wish to see in the world." And by being that change, we influence others to do the same.

Presence, like power, has always existed within us. In fact, presence is who we are when we strip away all that we are not. When our doubts and fears and illusions of fear-based beliefs are dissolved for good, then presence can be with us always. Presence enables us to experience leadership without experiencing the push and pull of agendas and motivations, and so is foundational to the wisdom teachings of the Tao. In Verse 4 of the *Tao Te Ching*, Lao Tzu says, "Tao is empty, yet it fills every vessel with endless supply. Tao is hidden, yet it shines in every corner of the universe."

The third pillar of influence is Purpose, of which there are two types. The first type is our soul's purpose, that is, what we have come here to do and the potential we've come to this world to fully express.

When we focus on fulfilling the mission of our purpose, we will either naturally influence others to take up our mission or we will inspire them to pursue and fulfill their own mission. In many cases, our journey will provide clarity to people who feel lost and without purpose themselves. The second type of purpose consists of the reason that we came to this earth—the bigger Divine Purpose we all share— which is to love. Period. No other purpose, but to love.

The final pillar of influence is Potential. What is possible for us, for others, and for our evolution as a species? How open are we to create a new reality? Albert Einstein once said, "I have no special talents. I am only passionately curious." Developing an openness to potential is a core component of being a change-maker. Please note that I did not say, "disrupter." In the Way of the Tao, leaders do not push, pull or destroy; they work in flow and harmony to create something new. When we are in creation energy—the energy of possibility—positive, lasting influence is more likely to occur.

The Four Pillars

- Power
- Presence
- Purpose
- Potential

Our relationships to potential, like power, presence, and purpose, are relationships that invite us to observe our thoughts, actions, and choices. Making space for potential, treating it as sacred, and asking for assistance from both your earthly team and your Divine Team is critical.

One of the least talked-about characteristics of powerful influencers is their reliance on Divine support—the unseen, the intangible, the mystical. When influencers speak of potential and possibility, they are visionaries asking us to see things that are not yet recognized by the human eye. They pull things into existence that were never there before, because they have faith in, and are working collaboratively with, Divine Power.

About This Book

As a part of my research for this book, I had the great pleasure of interviewing numerous global influencers, all of whom had something in common: their journeys were launched on a foundation of personal development. They each journeyed within first and came to know themselves through the process of self-examination. Bestselling author of *Mass Influence,* Teresa de Grosbois, said it this way: "The biggest turning point for me was the moment I made the decision to do my own personal development work. During that time, my business had failed, my marriage ended, and my health was in a tailspin. So, I had an idea to renovate my home, and as I was in the bathroom working on the tiles, the only thought I had was how utterly unhappy I was. I could not point to a time in the past ten years that made me feel happy. I decided that *I* needed to be renovated, not the bathroom. It was from that point forward that life slowly started to transform for me. Change had to start with me, and changing myself. You have to do the inner work to do the outer work."

This book guides you to do the inner work, in keeping with the principles of the Tao. Through these pages, you will have the opportunity to dedicate yourself to become a change-maker and influence others for the collective good. It may be challenging at times, but it is worth it. As Robert Frost put it, "It has made all the difference."

This book is designed to help you evolve your personal capacity for influence and empowerment and guide you to explore your potential both in the earthly realm and the Divine realm. Your ability to walk in both worlds is what I call the *Holy Flow*, which leads to enduring and infinite influence.

Within each chapter, you will discover how the ancient truths of the Tao can become your current reality. At the end of each chapter, you'll have an opportunity to reflect on, and take steps to integrate many of the profound teachings of the Tao into your life. Like all sacred teachings, each one is eternal and can sustain you consistently. When you apply them to the Four Pillars, using the practical, everyday processes in this book, you will discover a new state of influence: the Way of the Tao. In that state, people will feel your heart, soul, and your commitment, and be moved to act in ways that serve the greater good.

I will also describe how you can bring your mystical relationship with the Divine into much-needed action. We will explore mastery, and the ability to create at a high level. You might be motivated to begin or join a movement, for example, or to become an activist. As the *Tao Te Ching* often states, it is vital that our influence not be self-indulgent and expressed only within our own private desires. It's important to support the many people and the environment in ways that alleviate widespread suffering and destruction of all that is good.

The words "Tao Te Ching" mean "living and applying the Great Way." What is the Great Way? Scholars have debated that for centuries. But, since I will be referring to the Way of the Tao frequently throughout this book, the closest explanation I can offer is to say that it is the essence of love. The Tao speaks to what often gets in the way of love; the awareness of interruption in our natural state of love is at the heart of the Tao. And with awareness, comes transformation. I quote liberally from the *Tao Te Ching* (Translator, Jonathan Star) so that you can experience the Way of the Tao, influencing real and lasting change.

Pillar I

Power

One

Understanding Power

*The Sage helps all things come to know
the truth they have forgotten.*

—Tao Te Ching, Verse 64

Power is a mystery to most of us. People often think of it as either a positive or a negative force: something that can either destroy the planet or change the world for the greater good. One dictionary definition of power is: "The ability to influence a course of events or the behavior of others"—for better or for worse.

Throughout the many years of working with powerful people, I've come to recognize that the most significant outcome of power is the ability to influence. Yet influence can be fleeting and damaging if power is fueled by personal fear and egoic needs. We need not look far to see how that has played out. Greed, corruption, manipulation, and deceit are rampant among those who are driven by a need for power. They are constantly strategizing their next move to get something from someone or something. While many might consider these actions powerful, they are not an expression of true power because their influence is temporary. As the *Tao Te Ching* says in Verse 55, "Whatever is not Tao comes to an early end."

True power doesn't come from the mind or the ego. We cannot *think* our way to being powerful. True power originates in the love we are born with—the only energy form that creates true lasting influence. I call it *love-power* because of its infinite capacity to influence. Love-power cannot be contained by the ego or the mind. In fact, the mind has no capacity to contain even the smallest grain of infinite love. The job of the mind is to be our personal computer and collector of facts; it was never meant to be the source of our true power.

Yet Western civilization sees the mind as the source of power, confusing power with intellect. But the intellect is often intertwined with the ego, so love-based power often morphs into fear-based power, which I call *distorted power*. This is where destructive actions come from.

While popular self-help books refer to the term "losing your power," I don't believe we can ever lose it. However, we can distort the power we are born with and close off our access to our love-power. In other words, most of us begin life with our love-power quite active—we are happy, curious, in an unending state of awe, quick to forgive, and wide open to other people and to new opportunities. But, after a few years, we inevitably experience the fear or suspicion that we are not enough as we are. This suspicion leads to thoughts and emotions that become a set pattern of behaviors, which in turn become our state of being, taking us out of our inherent pure love-power and into fear-based, distorted power.

These patterns are so commonplace that many misinterpret negative power as "normal." Other than condemned, premeditated acts of violence, we often perceive control, domination and force as acceptable everyday behavior—behavior that has become normalized as "who we are," or worse yet, "who they are." For example, if we are quick to react to a text that we consider undesirable, we don't think of it as a misuse of our power, but as a justified tendency to be "hot-headed." When our natural power of love becomes distorted, we turn to trying to exert power—but as we do, we end up diminishing our own power just a little more. Each time we lower the energy of love, we close ourselves off to the only true source of true positive, influential power.

The field of quantum physics has now made speculations about energy a reality. In terms of measuring energy, our power vibrates fast or slow, depending on whether we have distorted our power or remain in our love-power. This is why we often feel that we are "losing our power." We feel less energy physically. We feel emotions that make us tired and weak, because we do the opposite of what we have come to the planet to express. This distortion of power is still a form of power, but it is a power that, over time, will lead to poor relationships, lack of health, and even lack of abundance in life.

In his ground-breaking book, *Power vs. Force*, David Hawkins calibrates the energy of each of the levels of human consciousness, on a scale ranging from one to a thousand, where one is mere existence, and one thousand is enlightenment. The calibration is based on a clinical science that emerged in the 1970s called *kinesiology*, which uses the body's muscles to indicate truth or falsehood (the body is strong with truth and weak with falsehood). Shame, guilt, apathy, grief, and fear all calibrate at one hundred or less because they are part of the falsehood or illusion that humans exist in. Love, joy, and peace calibrate between five and six hundred, as they represent the eternal Truth of who we are as Divine Beings in a human body. We begin to see the level of enlightened beings like Jesus and Buddha in the range of seven hundred. All levels of consciousness below two hundred are destructive, and all levels above two hundred are constructive. This gives us great insight into our relationship with power, because as we begin the journey to stay in our love-power, we are more and more attuned to the way in which our actions and thoughts impact our energy and the energy of those around us.

When we are in pure love-power, those around us are influenced merely by being in our presence. On the other hand, distorted power

can bring many people down with us, or we can feel down when
someone begins to turn from love-power to fear-based power. Have
you ever experienced a meeting with several fearful people and felt
exhausted later? Have you ever spent an afternoon with a complaining
friend and ended up going straight to bed or decided against doing
that productive task you intended to do when you got home? If so,
you've experienced the energetic consequences of distorted power.

When distorted power meets love-power, it is outmatched. Hawkins
says that one person living in the highest vibrations of consciousness
is enough to counteract seventy million individuals living in the
lowest vibrations. That is, the power of one person living in pure,
unconditional love (calibrating at approximately five hundred)
can counteract 750,000 individuals living below level two hundred,
the borderline of destructive consciousness. The greatest form of
influence—the most impactful, positive effect—comes from living in
heightened states of consciousness, where your being tangibly impacts
the consciousness of the world.

Distorted power can be so ingrained in our everyday way of being
that we don't recognize it in our words and actions. Acting as a victim
or martyr is an expression of distorted power; engaging in passive-
aggressive behavior is a use of distorted power; insisting that your
way is the only way is distorted power at work. Distorted power can
also take the form of careless behavior, risking everything to feel
special and noticed, and demanding the universe and its inhabitants
take notice. Not following through on your word, showing up late
for events, sharing unkind words about another being—all of these
are expressions of distorted power. All of it can bring you down in
an instant.

The Laws of Nature

But how do we shift from culturally condoned patterns of expressing distorted power to expressing our true love-power? To overcome our habit of being stuck in an energetically low level of power and free ourselves to activate the radiant love-power within, we can look to Mother Nature for simple teachings that can be helpful to this kind of personal evolution.

True power is ruled by the laws of nature, so understanding them lays the groundwork for us to experience a pure relationship with power. The laws of nature are impersonal; they exist whether any person or life form wants them to or not. They are also universal—they apply to one and all—the natural world as well as humanity.

When we are aware of the laws of nature but still violate them, we distort our power, reduce our vital energy, and lose track of happiness. After all, disagreeing with the laws of nature—irrefutable as they are— cannot produce fulfillment, joy, peace, or sustainable relationships. Yet, most of us fall into the trap of expressing distorted power every day. Except maybe the Dalai Lama. (There's always an exception!)

The three laws of nature that have the greatest impact on our relationship with power and our growth as an influencer are the Law of Change, the Law of Letting Go, and the Law of the Impersonal.

The three laws of nature

- Law of Change

- Law of Letting Go

- Law of the Impersonal

THE LAW OF CHANGE

Accept difficulty as opportunity.

—Tao Te Ching, Verse 63

Nothing in life stays the same. Nature flows with cycles of change. Plants and animals live in a constant state of growth, decay, and rebirth. Humans are the only species that resist change—especially whatever they interpret as difficult change. We believe this or that "should not" happen. With the onset of the 2020 pandemic, we can see that those who accept and adjust to their circumstances are more influential, peaceful, and fulfilled.

Our love-power is freed up when we accept and work with the Law of Change. Influential people with a high degree of love-power know that lasting influence is not maintained without attention to this law. Jesus, Buddha, Mother Teresa, Martin Luther King, and Gandhi each served at the highest level for the good of all by adhering to the Law of Change. These people had comforts of home and family and, in some cases, considerable wealth, but listened to a deeper calling to set out on a path that would change the future of humanity in profound ways.

Undoubtedly, change was not easy for these leaders; there were times when they, too, resisted change. Yet their perseverance altered the course of humanity. The irony is that when we resist a fundamental law such as the Law of Change, the short-term resistance might feel like a relief, but we suffer in the long run. We can feel sadness, anger, or a host of other emotions. We often turn outward, blaming, complaining, and repeating the same story or circumstances to others. When we point fingers of blame at the outer world, it's generally because we're not accepting the Law of Change in our inner world.

Recognizing the Law of Change in our physical reality is also helpful. When I tell people I recently turned fifty, I find it humorous to see how people react. "You don't look fifty!" is one of the typical consolation prizes offered up. Others are speechless, exuding a quiet sympathy. Still others offer products to help me look younger and reduce the increasing number of wrinkles appearing on my face. While I have come to love and accept my body at this time in my life, most people don't share this sentiment. For most reaching their second half of life, fear of aging suddenly takes hold. But what has your body been doing for the last few decades, if not changing? The body must, within the laws of nature, go through cycles of change, constantly and dependably.

When people resist the Law of Change on the physical plane, they join the ever-growing number of people who chase after external sources of satisfaction to avoid having to change. They have compulsive urges to buy things, reinvent their looks, renovate their homes, and more. They become obsessed with making money to manipulate their external environment so they can maintain an illusion of a safe world they can control—what they can change according to *their* time frame and preferences. In other words, they are creating the *illusion* of change as they try to avoid and resist the change that is being asked of them internally.

Here's the rub: when people don't change, they are more easily controlled and manipulated. The powers that be are well aware of this, too, make no mistake. For example, it only takes a stroll through the average North American shopping mall or an online shopping hub to realize how deeply entrenched we are in the culture and habits of buying. But if you can unplug from the thousands of daily offerings supporting an addictive fix—temptations that temporarily help you feel okay about yourself so that you don't have to undertake real change—you'll experience a massive leap in consciousness.

When physical changes like new clothes, new hair, a facelift, a house renovation, a new car, or a new phone quickly prove to be a fleeting satisfaction, people may enter a dark period where they feel empty, lost, directionless, or without purpose. Many feel the pain of the bandage of buying. They spend their lives living out the dreams of others because they haven't developed a practice of listening to and acting upon the whispers of change within.

When we accept the Law of Change and recognize that all things come and go, we activate the courage within to make necessary changes that empower true power and influence. The Tao is essentially about allowing the flow of life to flourish, without resistance, and to bring us the wisdom and inner guidance that accompany it.

THE LAW OF LETTING GO

The treasure of life is missed by those who
hold on and gained by those who let go.

—*Tao Te Ching, Verse 75*

In nature, everything has a beginning and an end, a cycle of birth and death, decay, and renewal. For these cycles to continue unimpeded, nature needs to release the old to make way for the new. This principle, of course, is closely tied to the Law of Change. Yet the Law of Letting Go deserves as much attention because of how it shapes the universe and everything in it.

Let's take a look.

In nature, plants that hold on to dead or dying flowers have less energy than those that quickly let go of flowers that have completed their life cycle. In the garden, dead-heading plants helps them last longer and produce even more flowers. If flowers that have finished blooming are not released, the plant no longer thrives. The energy of the plant is revitalized when the old has been released. This shows us that energy itself does not grow old; energy just gets blocked and stuffed down by any form of resistance to letting go.

Similarly, your life force, your love-power, is impacted each time you hang on to old grievances or even recent ones. It's also affected when you hold on to people you were once in relationship with or those who have passed over. Your love-power turns into distorted power the moment you hang on to anyone or anything, even as our collective illusion convinces us that what was good should never go away. Or, that if you let go, then you have lost. Or, if you let go, then you must be unworthy, less than, or unlovable. Or, there must be something wrong with you. So, you hold on to what is ultimately siphoning off your energy, in spite of the truth.

Most people will do anything to avoid seeing the beliefs that control them. But by resisting the Law of Letting Go, they avoid looking at the illusions and beliefs they've built their life upon, the biggest of which is, "There must be something wrong with me if I have to let go of something that was once so good. I must have made a mistake that proves I'm unworthy." Most of us hang on to our baggage only to begin a search for answers as to why we are unhappy. We may blame others; in fact, chances are good that we will point fingers to something or someone that is stopping us from moving on.

Relationships are one of the most difficult things to let go of. I'm not referring to the act of divorce or separation, although that may be an end result. I'm referring to letting go of the unhealthy energetic ties that we have built up with a person that we are or were in an intimate relationship with.

One of the most profound relationships of my life, and one I will always cherish, was with a man I met after my marriage fell apart.

For the eight years we were together, he gave me emotional support when I was punishing myself over a failed marriage. He comforted me when I was sad or angry about yet another issue concerning my former husband—the man I spent almost two decades of my life with. But my optimistic view of the new relationship was flawed from the beginning—I resisted the truisms of the Law of Letting Go.

I had been carrying a lot of blame, anger, and guilt—mostly toward myself—for many years after my divorce. I refused to love myself, and I resisted letting go of my numerous negative beliefs about myself as a wife and mother. So, guess what I attracted? A rescuer! The classic archetypical pairing of the wounded bird (me) who meets the rescuer (him). For a while, I felt soothed by the resurrected belief that I was loveable, and he felt temporarily worthwhile because he could help someone in need. The dynamic played out for years. I felt trapped by my circumstances, stuck in victim mode, and only accepted help that didn't really move me forward. Then things really went sour. I became increasingly unhappy, pointing the finger outward, and he felt resentment that he was not being acknowledged for his assistance, which then turned into passive-aggressive behavior. We both wondered, "Why can't they be more like me?" No surprise how it ended.

By resisting the Law of Letting Go, both of us were not stepping into new opportunities to grow and live our full potential. Our energies were invested in hanging on to our unhealthy needs and our ego desires to protect ourselves from not being enough. Most people stay in this kind of resistance and hang on to old habits, behaviors, circumstances, and relationships for years, if not decades. But true influence can't happen when we resist letting go, in any areas of our lives. Others sense that we're not living our authentic truth, not genuinely present.

What do you need to release? What are you hanging on to that no longer serves you? What power struggle are you engaged in that drives you to stay exactly where you are as you store all your mental and emotional baggage of the past? How does the way in which you see the world distort your natural and pure love? The Buddha said that we see through the eyes of fear, and this perspective becomes so real that we forget we are living an illusion. The minute we are trapped by the illusion of fear and the needs of the ego, we buy into the illusion, and it becomes seemingly impossible to let go, surrender, and be in the flow of life that is the Tao.

THE LAW OF THE IMPERSONAL

The Sage is like Heaven and Earth. To him, none are especially dear.

—*Tao Te Ching, Verse 5*

Several years ago, I had the privilege of taking human behavioral specialist Dr. John Demartini and a friend sightseeing in beautiful Vancouver, British Columbia, my homeland. It was a nippy spring morning, and as the hours went by, I noticed that no matter what we discussed or what we encountered that day, John was absolutely grounded in peace, stillness, and overall happiness. Even when we spoke of tragic personal events, he didn't alter his state. I had never met anyone like him before, and I realized that he was living the Way of the Tao and embodying the Law of the Impersonal. He didn't see any individual event as better or worse than any other. And as a result, he didn't suffer. He put it this way, "Suffering is expecting the world to be only one way and then being surprised when it's not."

Nature is a great role model for us when it comes to the Law of the Impersonal. Nature does not hold anyone or anything "especially dear." It does not give to only a few, nor does it protect just a few from tragic natural occurrences. Nature does what it does, whether it's a fire, a flood, a tornado, or a new life. Nature simply creates and destroys. Humans are the only creatures on the planet that take every act, word, and thought personally. Most of us feel we cannot exist in an impersonal world. Even when it comes to concepts of the Divine, most of us take it personally, and that is why we suffer. Believing that if we are good, then bad things won't happen, we are surprised to realize that no matter if our behavior is good or bad, "good" and "bad" things will happen. No one is immune. It's not personal.

In my own life, a dear friend passed of cancer, leaving behind young children, three of my clients passed away in the past few months, and the son of a friend just died in an auto accident. It's tempting to ask, "Why?" In our Western world, we worship our intellect as having all the answers to life. Our civilization has come up with the answers to most everything, so why not this, too? We want to know why. But it's not personal.

Two animals died in my backyard this summer. I was shaken to see the remains of a rabbit attacked and killed by a hawk. A week later, a bird hit my front window in the early morning, and I watched it die within seconds of falling to the ground. I felt helpless. There was nothing I could do to stop it. Tears welled up in my eyes as my prayer to return this bird to life "failed." So often, we want to control what we perceive as "not good," even when it has to do with death, and even when we know that death is part of life. It is a natural law; all that is living will die. And yet we resist. We suffer. But it's not personal.

Our refusal to accept the impersonal nature of life can increase our suffering and contribute to the distortion of our power. Instead of allowing ourselves to feel the emotion of sadness, we become bitter, for example. We dwell on the same unanswerable questions over and over: Why did this have to happen in my family? Why are we cursed while others are so blessed? Some give up on God. Some decide not to grow or evolve. Some people sever their relationships with others and stop pursuing new ones. When we take the impersonal personally, our positive influence comes to a halt. Taking it all personally, some people end up feeling sorry for themselves, considering themselves to be the perpetual victim, and telling their sad story to anyone who will listen. Others become full of rage and hurt others with their words and actions. All of this suffering occurs only because they demand that a personal universe give them reasons for why things happen as they do.

Part of the disconnect is simply because the mind is a reasoning tool that cannot comprehend how the same Source that loves and supports us doesn't consider us special at the same time. It doesn't make any effort to treat us as special. For most, it is incomprehensible.

When I'm guiding budding entrepreneurs to share their message and sell their products and programs, I remind them that one of the best mindsets in business is to learn to expect and accept challenges as they arise. This is not about being pessimistic; it is creating a foundation for the acceptance of natural laws. It's not a matter of *if* those challenges will happen, it's *when*. That perspective empowers people to withstand challenges, not out of fear, but out of love.

What it comes down to is this: expectations will immediately or eventually bring suffering. The need to always have things turn out the way we expect will ultimately create unhappiness; the unmet expectations then turn love-power into distorted power. Harboring expectations fuels the ego's ploys to make us feel safe, to let us see only the threats in life, to look for refuge in what we have, to get what we want—rather than look for challenges and risk losing what we have to evolve or grow.

When people take the world personally and don't like the cards they're dealt, they blame others, God or the Universe, for things not going their way. Some people become aggressive as they try to control the outcomes, insisting that they are special and deserve special treatment. This 'specialness' builds into a sense of entitlement—a common form of distorted power. Feeling entitled, they perceive that the universe, their community, and the people in their lives owe them something. It's all a result of the inability to see the impersonal nature of life.

The solution? Stop using your mind to figure things out. Fully accept the Law of the Impersonal, this intrinsic law of nature, and accept the entirety of what life brings. As Lao Tzu wrote, "Sometimes you're behind, other times ahead, sometimes strong, other times weak, sometimes with, other times alone; to the Sage, the movement of life is perfection."

Reflections

Draw your attention to how your ego fights your acceptance of your current situation and the present moment. (And it will—every day.) Combine this attention with the daily practice of gratitude. Learn to see every moment as a moment of grace. Gradually the acceptance of an impersonal world will become more commonplace than the ego's fight for specialness and personal meaning.

Choose a new favorite journal to begin recording insights from your journey with *The Tao of Influence*. Like this one, each chapter will close with an opportunity for you to reflect on and integrate your learnings.

Ask yourself: Which of the three laws of nature do you flow well with? Which one do you feel most at peace with? How does the acceptance of this law enrich your life? How has your acceptance of this law affected those around you? What steps can you take to help others activate this law of nature in their own lives?

Ask yourself: Which of the three laws of nature do you resist? How has your resistance to the law contributed to your personal suffering? How has your resistance to it affected the lives of those around you? What steps can you take to more fully accept this law of nature and let it flow in your life?

Two

Identifying Your Power Patterns

Only when your sickness becomes sick
will your sickness disappear.

—Tao Te Ching, Verse 71

Understanding your power and noticing where your power gets distorted is essential to identifying patterns of power. In my years as a trainer in human potential and consciousness, I've come to notice eight basic power patterns that develop over time and become distorted versions of power. They are so common that we don't notice that they prevent us from impacting and influencing the world for the better; in fact, they are considered normal enough to most people that they continue to play out unconsciously for years and even whole lifetimes. Why do these power patterns persist, in spite of the fact that they are frustrating, irritating, lacking in connection, and unproductive? They endure because they are considered to be a natural part of the human makeup. But don't believe it for a second. There is nothing natural or normal about distorting what you are—the energy and essence of love.

As Lao Tzu says in the *Tao Te Ching*, to tap into that energy of love, you have to recognize the sickness and get so fed up with living in a prison of dis-ease that you are willing to do whatever it takes to live free. By becoming more aware of the sickness, and releasing blocks to your true power, you become less willing to accept the "sickness" as normal, and you're empowered to make new choices. The greatest positive influencers in the world impacted millions simply because they would not accept what others considered as normal. They offered an alternative that challenged people's outdated ways of being and thinking. That's the way of a true influencer.

The Eight Power Patterns

Having done the groundwork of understanding what power is in the last chapter, the next step is to understand why you have developed your power patterns in the first place. By recognizing your personal power patterns and default ways of interacting with the world, you'll begin to loosen their grip over you and free yourself to access deeper, more authentic power.

Consider this. Before birth, you are a fetus floating around in a comfortable, warm bath, happily doing your thing. Then, one day, you are suddenly forced out of your safe environment and, like a fish out of water, you gasp for life. Your little lungs, much to your surprise, start taking in air. You open your eyes and see hundreds and then thousands of different impressions.

We are born into a world of distraction. The sensory, chaotic circus that we are born into completely overwhelms the brain, which goes into a state of confusion. So, you cry in distress. Then the brain tries to balance things out by focusing on a few things, especially the smiling face of a parent or caretaker. Now, finally, you can relax, and your brain begins to shape its understanding of the world.

You begin to focus on the familiar faces, and as you do, you notice that certain things you do cause those faces, and the voices coming from those faces, to respond to you in ways that make you feel good. And certain things they don't do make you feel bad. All you want to do is feel good, so you make choices that ensure that will happen. This is when power patterns begin: as you learn to manipulate the environment to feel good. Still, everyone loves you for it, and for the most part, they are patient and understanding. They recognize that baby is merely acting from a place of wanting its needs met.

As you grow, you still want the faces and voices in your life to feel good. And when they don't feel good, you make it mean that something is wrong with you. After all, you know how to make yourself feel good, so why can't you make others feel good too? Sometimes you hear or see evidence that you are not okay. You might hear an adult say that you could be doing something differently or should be this way and not that way. And you believe the opinions and preferences of these adults because they are like God to you.

Once we develop the suspicion that there is something wrong with us and that we are not okay, most of us will spend the rest of our lives trying to cover it up. We try to put a bandage on our wounds by manipulating our environment and the people around us so that we can feel good about ourselves. We try different tactics—some work and some don't—but we go with the ones that work because we are smart. As we discover the ones that work best, we gravitate toward certain power patterns. This is where it begins. Disguised as "personality traits," our power patterns are constantly fortified by the fear that we are not enough, not worthy, not loveable, and generally not okay. For example, when we exhibit the need to control our environment or the need to be right, adults might call us "determined" or "stubborn." When we exhibit withdrawal as our signature way to cope, we are the "quiet one."

The good news is that we can change our power patterns; we don't have to be stuck with them. To do so, your first step is to identify the power patterns that have the most control over you.

The eight power patterns listed below are the ones that are most common. Read through them and find out where you see yourself. As you do this, I invite you to be completely honest with yourself. The degree to which you are willing to look at yourself and acknowledge the power patterns you use is the degree to which you will grow as a conscious influencer, creating real and lasting positive change on the planet.

1. The Controller

A person with the Controller power pattern is fueled by the fear that he or she is not, and will never be, enough. They believe that no one can be trusted, and the universe is not safe. The Controller will not only dominate conversations by interrupting, talking over others, and insisting on the last word, but they will also control through passive-aggressive "silent treatment," running away from conflict, and showing up late for meetings. The Controller can be both aggressive and passive-aggressive in the same day; they often play both sides well to reach their goal, which is to be safe and to protect against perceived betrayal and criticism.

The Controller has rigid expectations of what life should look like. They believe that people need to think and behave according to their rulebook—and it's a large one! The Controller has rules that carry heavy expectations of how relationships ought to look, how work ought to progress, and how society ought to behave. Most of us carry some expectations that we don't even know exist. Yet when we become unhappy, irritated, or even mildly annoyed with someone or some event, it's because we've carried expectations. In Verse 7 of the *Tao Te*

Ching, we are reminded that "the Sage puts his own views behind and so ends up ahead. He stays a witness to life, so he endures."

While expectations are a big part of the Controller pattern, it's important to note that not all expectations are bad. If two or more people create a clear agreement pertaining to expectations, and it is based on trust, integrity, and follow-through, then expectations can lead to harmony and peace. But every so often, it is healthy to reexamine and challenge these expectations to make sure they are still working for all involved. However, most expectations are based on a desire to control an outcome or a person, and this desire can have a catastrophic impact on relationships and even entire companies if not kept in check.

There's a fine line between healthy intentions and the expectations that distort pure power. When an intention or goal is set and activated, become clear on your role and responsibility in seeing it come into creation. Be aware of the energy you put into imagining how others will behave and what they must do for you to reach your goal.

Nowhere is this more apparent than at the beginning of a romantic relationship. Often, when people get excited about meeting each other and finally clicking with that "special someone," they create visualizations and thoughts about what that person will do or say with the outcome being lifelong happiness. They begin to expect certain words to be said, certain actions to be fulfilled, certain beliefs to become apparent. And when these expectations are not met, the relationship becomes tainted by feelings and behaviors demonstrating righteousness, withdrawal, victim perspective, superiority, and a host of other power patterns that quickly extinguish any possibility for the relationship to thrive. For a relationship not to be dominated by the Controller, constant vigilance around expectations is critical.

In his bestselling book, *The Untethered Soul*, Michael Singer speaks to the false sense of control that expectations are built on:

> Your mind has very little control over this world. It is neither omniscient nor omnipotent. It cannot control the weather and other natural forces. Nor can it control all people, places, and things around you. You have given your mind an impossible task by asking it to manipulate the world to fix your personal inner problems. If you want to achieve a healthy state of being, stop asking your mind to do this. Just relieve your mind of the job of making sure that everyone and everything will be the way you need them to be so that you can feel better inside. Your mind is not qualified for that job. Fire it and let go of your inner problems instead.

The need to protect ourselves generates a complexity of problems that we then have to deal with. When we let go of the Controller within, remove our focus on protecting ourselves, and open to the flow of life—the Way of the Tao—we begin a life of freedom and expansion.

RELEASING THE CONTROLLER PATTERN

If we are to be more than just a mind and body, but a spirit living on the earth, if we want to allow ourselves to be guided and stop pushing our way through life without deep sacred reflection, then we need to work at releasing the Controller power pattern. As a result, we begin to feel more free and joyful in our pure power.

To help people let go of the tendency to rely on their minds to try to control their environment and inner world, I often advise them to drop into what I call their "Inner Teacher." The Controller desperately resists the Inner Teacher and the call of the soul. It ignores or dismisses intuitive guidance because intuition is, by nature, a change-agent. Intuition demands that we look at our lives and make the changes necessary to move forward. The Controller tries to shut out intuition, so that it has no competing forces on the way to its goal. Have you ever set a goal for yourself, only to realize when you got there that it wasn't really what you wanted? Your intuition was speaking to you the entire time, but your Controller aspect was dominant.

Begin by using your awareness. Start to notice the feelings you have inside right before you turn to the Controller within. Notice what triggered you to act out this power pattern. Notice what beliefs you have about yourself and the world around you that initiated the trigger. Journal extensively so that you can stop your behavior and thought process when they turn from love-power to the distorted power of the Controller. When you see your power patterns for what they are, you can never un-see them. When you recognize the pattern in action, stop and remind yourself that you choose to release it.

Say to yourself something helpful, like: "I train my mind; my mind does not train me."

There are many ways the Controller power pattern expresses itself. Here's a list that can help you recognize the Controller in you:

> *"You should do this."*
> *"I can't believe this is happening."*
> *"Don't use that word with me."*
> *"Come here right now."*
> *"Just stop it."*
> *"Really?"*
> *"You listen to me!"*
> *"I'm the boss in this house."*
> *"How dare she say that to me!"*

Controller feelings might also show up as anger, irritation, screaming or yelling at another, or explosive energy rising. These feelings are usually generated from a fear that is related to safety or overall wellbeing.

I have noticed the Controller power pattern in myself. It often emerged when it was important for me to be right about something that I cared about. For example, after turning vegan, I began to notice family and friends' eating habits and started commenting on their unhealthy food choices. "You shouldn't be eating that," I'd say, thinking I was making a loving comment. After all, I figured, I could be saving their life from a heart attack due to cholesterol and high blood pressure! But I later realized that my demands were not coming from love, but from a fear that I developed when my dad died. By the time I was sixteen, my dad had become a heavy smoker. When I'd go to visit my parents as a young adult, I'd remind my dad occasionally to cut down on his smoking. Years later, when he died at the age of sixty-nine from liver cancer, I berated myself, thinking I could have done more to stop his early death. And I unconsciously created a belief that if I let people be who they are, they will leave me.

After my dad passed, the Controller in me became stronger than ever before. I lost close friends and connection with my kids. People were afraid to get too close to me as they could feel the energy of it just being around me. I've since released a lot of the Controller within me, but every so often, I am still surprised how this power pattern creeps up and takes hold. Only when I could see it playing out and see the fear that drove the power pattern was I able to put a stop to it.

Singer also speaks to the tendency for people to constantly protect themselves, a signature trait of the Controller: "This tendency exists because you truly have no control, and that is not comfortable to you. But if you really want to break through, you have to be willing to just watch the fear without protecting yourself from it."

Defensiveness is a sure sign of Controller energy. Having to defend your opinions and defend who you are is exhausting and depletes you of energy. To disengage this power pattern, remain open to the fear, including the thoughts and emotions moving through you; avoid closing your heart and allow yourself to feel fear as an ocean wave that arrives and then dissipates. Just like a wave, it can naturally calm to nothingness.

2. The Victim

Someone with the Victim power pattern lives from a fear that they are not, and never will be, loveable. They buy into the belief that life is hard, and that life is unfair. Victims tend to tell the same story repeatedly to demonstrate that life is hard—and to get a little bit of loving sympathy! The Victim has three main roles. The first role is to try to keep the individual—and everyone, for that matter—resisting the three laws of nature, as we discussed in Chapter One. Its secondary role is to ensure that all baggage from the past is not left behind, because it needs to keep us believing that we are not loveable—and the proof is in the pudding! Its third role is to take everything personally, resisting the second law of nature. The Victim is very sensitive to the words and actions of others, and so can become the greatest of storytellers and gossipers. They often take on passive-aggressive behavior until the energy of the bottled-up thoughts and emotions explode, often giving them a semblance of external control since they cannot control their inner world.

The Victim is a chronic complainer. Their perspective is that everything is done to them, not for them. Victim language is everywhere; it is so pervasive that most of us think that it's normal to talk and think this way. Some common Victim phrases sound like:

> *"I never have enough time."*
> *"He will never change."*
> *"I never have time for me."*
> *"The weather has got me down."*
> *"I'm just so busy."*

Victim words both resist what is and abdicate responsibility, placing blame on something or someone else.

RELEASING THE VICTIM PATTERN

Fortunately, Victim energy can be diffused through the practice of gratitude. Ask yourself: "What am I thankful for in this moment? In this moment, am I seeing a worldview that is filled with fear, negativity, and hopelessness? Can I see love, positivity, and possibility instead?" The Victim energy is strong in many people, and the only way out of it is to practice noticing the stories and complaints you tell yourself. When you do, immediately stop—mid-thought or mid-sentence—and disengage from the thought or story, replacing it with present-moment gratitude.

Replace Victim language with words that show gratitude, connection, love, and joy. For example, replace, "He will never change" with "I accept him for who he is, and I'm grateful for what I've learned about myself in this relationship." Having gratitude doesn't necessarily mean that you agree with the actions or values of another, but you see how everyone comes into your life to assist in your soul's journey. Things happen *for* you, not *to* you. As Eckhart Tolle said, "If I accept the fact that my relationships are here to make me conscious, instead of happy, then my relationships become a wonderful self-mastery tool that keeps realigning me with my higher purpose for living."

Being grateful for someone who hurt you can be difficult. But keep in mind that influencers use their wounds to elevate their own consciousness by creating miracles for others. They use difficult times to pass on wisdom to others and to create new ideas or products that help future generations. By choosing words carefully and by replacing the Victim power pattern with gratitude, you walk the Tao of Influence.

3. The Savior

I have witnessed this pattern many times; it is one I've admired for its desire to do good and support others. The Savior power pattern often moves the world forward with heroic actions and deeds. People with Savior tendencies are great at problem-solving and take pride in alleviating people's problems. However, this power pattern hides behind the fear that sounds like this: "I am not enough and will never be enough no matter how hard I try and how many people I help." Because this fear underlies the actions of Saviors, they experience a "hit" of pleasure along with feel-good endorphins when they're saving someone, but, like those addicted to substances, they are left feeling empty and craving the attention and accolades of their good deeds to fill themselves up. The *Tao Te Ching* says, "Give without condition and the people will prosper. Want nothing and the people will find everything." A Savior believes this is what they are doing, yet the change they attempt to create cannot sustain itself with the wound they carry beneath the surface. As a result, their influence is minimal and short-lived.

Nowhere is the Savior more evident than in intimate relationships. Typically, the masculine energy wants to fix things, and so it goes about looking for opportunities to do so. That desire affixes itself to the Savior power pattern, resulting in a rescuing situation. If the "masculine" has the power pattern of Savior, it will always get its satisfaction from rescuing the "feminine" in the relationship. Yet, as with all externally motivated behavior, the Savior cannot sustain satisfaction and soon feels unfulfilled once again.

Saviors often choose people with a Victim pattern for their intimate partner. Why? Because Victims want to be rescued from their pain. Unfortunately, the two power patterns cannot survive the dynamic because neither is based in love. The Savior needs to prove that they are enough, and the Victim needs to prove that he or she is never enough. The Victim won't feel complete and will complain about the Savior; the Savior will get jaded after several attempts to save don't get sufficiently acknowledged or received by the Victim. Even when there is an attempt at gratitude, it is short-lived, since the Victim is more invested in their story than in getting help to get out of the story. The Savior is more invested in proving self-worth than in discovering self-love.

RELEASING THE SAVIOR PATTERN

The first step to dissolving the Savior energy is to make a commitment to witness your strong tendency to rescue and to be drawn to Victim behavior. It's also important to observe and notice the language of the Savior pattern. Here are some words that Saviors often say, along with what they're thinking:

> *"I'll help you"* (*...even if you haven't requested help.*)

> *"I took out the garbage."* (*...and I expect to be acknowledged.*)

> *"Don't worry. I've got this handled."* (*...If it wasn't for me, things would fall apart around here.*)

> *"I've got the answer."* (*...There's only one solution, and I have it!*)

Because the Savior's worldview is external, it always tries to fill itself up with the help of external sources: by being seen, being appreciated, and being rewarded. When that fails, the Savior often takes on a secondary power pattern—the Martyr.

4. The Martyr

This power pattern is obvious to everyone except for the Martyrs themselves. They genuinely believe that their kind, loving, supportive role comes from selfless and enduring love. The Martyr takes on the burden of responsibility and then proceeds to complain about it to anyone who will listen. (Or, they will nobly repress their true feelings and become ill or even manifest a disease.) I've attended many funerals where the eulogy focuses on the martyr qualities of the deceased: "Mary was a giver. She gave to everyone she knew, and even though she would run herself ragged and be exhausted, she was still out there serving pancakes to the hungry and knitting mittens for the poor children on the block." I'm not suggesting that we shouldn't think of others; in fact, the Tao encourages us to radiate our love-power into the world by serving others. However, we rarely emphasize the attributes of joy, pleasure, and self-care. Eulogies rarely refer to the deceased in this way: "One fantastic thing about Mary was that she knew how to take care of herself, love herself and have a joyful, pleasure-filled life."

The Martyr rarely takes time for themself and doesn't take a moment to enjoy for the sake of joy. This is because the Martyr buys into the belief that their role on earth is to suffer and endure. They will find every opportunity, including volunteer roles (where they feel unappreciated of course) to confirm this belief. The Martyr, like the Victim, resists all three laws of nature, and so is one of the most difficult patterns to release. It is highly entrenched in staying stuck in the glorious burden of responsibility.

RELEASING THE MARTYR PATTERN

To effectively navigate Martyr energy, keep a list of the things you say every day that indicate that this power pattern has control over you. Some common phrases the Martyr may be inclined to use are:

"No one else will do it, so I have to."
"I'm always picking up the pieces."
"Someone has to do it."

"I'm just so tired these days."
"I do so much for so little."
"They are relying on me."
"I'm wearing too many hats, but there's no way out."

Notice these statements are focused on the problem and not the solution. When you feel yourself going into the Martyr energy, ask yourself, "What am I prepared to do about this situation?" The Martyr's key to survival is to suffer, so if you want to rid yourself of this power pattern, you must make the choice (at first daily) to take action toward what you do want.

5. The Blamer

The Blamer power pattern is linked to the Controller since its primary motivation is to protect us from the belief that we are not enough. The Blamer externalizes events, which gives us a sense of control and righteousness about life and people. When we blame, we get to be right. We have the last word. We get to justify our own unhappiness. Essentially, the Blamer makes everyone else wrong because they have not met our needs or followed our rulebook for life.

The energy of the Blamer pattern can be so seductive that it can arise as a power dynamic in boardrooms, living rooms, and bedrooms— any time people feel unsafe to make mistakes, be authentic, and tell the truth. Not surprisingly, Blamer energy attracts betrayal and lies. Influencers should attend to this trait first, since it can make the difference between the ability to establish equitable power in social and professional settings or create a place of mistrust, suppression, and a host of other symptoms that end in energetic "divorce." I recommend that every boardroom and bedroom display this Rumi quote as a reminder: "Out beyond ideas of wrongdoing and rightdoing, there is a field. I will meet you there." Rumi shared a great truth: only when we set down our addiction to blame will we fully enter a field of possibility.

The Blamer also runs on the dynamic of transactions based on "if." "If you do this, I will be happy." "If you don't say this, I will feel comfortable." The Blamer has an enormous rulebook of how people ought to behave, both on a personal and global level. This inevitably leads to unhappiness, since the world will never obey our every command or align with all of our personal rules.

RELEASING THE BLAMER PATTERN

The first step to dissolving the Blamer energy is to make a commitment to never again blame another person for the choices that you make. Promise yourself to never again utter words that imply that you are not 100 percent responsible for your life. Don't feed the notion that something or someone else is responsible for your thoughts, feelings, beliefs, or actions. Commit to stopping this kind of behavior now, and you will begin to experience true inner peace and joy.

Become like a watchdog: vigilant to the moment you think or say words that indicate blame. Stop mid-sentence or mid-thought and replace that blame with words that are the true source of your power. For example, if you think, "She never makes up her mind and expects me to make all the decisions for her." Say out loud, "STOP." Feel the love you have in that moment for the person. What do you love about her? Perhaps it's one word: kindness. You could say, "She is kind and loving to my kids and to me. I do not wish to change her; I only wish to change me. I let go of all blame now." Saying this frees you from the vicious never-ending cycle that blame creates. Above all, influencers are free people. They don't hold on to the energy of blame; rather, they consistently move forward in the spirit of creating a better world.

If you have felt enormous betrayal in your life, and you feel justified to blame someone, ask yourself, "Why didn't I listen to my intuition about this? What inside me refused to receive the clear intuition that was available to me all along?" If the betrayal occurred when you were a child, acknowledge that you did not have the resources to cope, and that now that you are grown, you can access resources to support you in dealing with trauma, so that you no longer use your vital energy toward blame and bitterness. When you take action and make the commitment to never blame another again, you will be well on your way to releasing this power pattern.

6. The Judge

The Judge power pattern often follows the Blamer energy, but in addition to blaming, the Judge adopts the role of observer and assessor of human actions and interactions. The judge then deems the action or interaction to be right/wrong, good/bad, smart/dumb, worthy/ unworthy, loveable/unloveable. This is because the Judge lives in a world of duality, where everything is assessed rather than accepted. Judge energy not only condemns or exalts others, it focuses on observing our every move and thought, taking great care to jump in and point out when we have not followed its rulebook.

The Judge power pattern keeps us separate from others and our true self. We can't have meaningful, present, and loving conversations and relationships if we judge. Wayne Dyer said, "Love is the ability and willingness to allow those that you care for to be what they choose for themselves without any insistence that they satisfy you." Quite the opposite, Judge energy doesn't allow freedom; it traps people into feeling less-than at best, and at worst, guilty and ashamed.

Even if we don't voice our judgments and never take on Blamer energy, if the Judge is inside, others will feel it and don't want to be around us. And even if they do put up with it, everyone ends up playing a game of "frenemy." That is, we may be friends when we're face-to-face, but we gossip about one another like enemies when given the opportunity. The best way to be in your pure love energy, which is your ultimate source of power and influence, is to relinquish the Judge. Make a commitment to never verbalize another bad word about anyone. That may be a challenge, but each time we are tempted, we remind ourselves to simply allow people to be who they are.

You might be thinking: "I do allow, and I do accept!" I thought the same thing about myself until I had the courage to look more deeply. First, I noticed that I judged people who were loud and conflict-oriented, those who were harsh with words and quick to judge. Somewhat ironic! This was my "shadow" side. I was blind to the fact that my judgment had nothing to do with them and everything to do with the fact that the Judge lived in me. I judged myself for all the times that I chose conflict rather than a loving path. I couldn't accept my own harshness toward people in my family, so I looked outward to condemn the harshness of others. What I didn't like in others was exactly what I didn't like about myself.

I remember an Ah-ha! moment when I recognized the Judge within. It happened while I was on vacation with my kids. My oldest son, Matthew, was eight years old, and I was constantly frustrated by his behavior. I couldn't understand his choices and wished he would just be an easygoing and agreeable child. Halfway into the vacation, my anger exploded, and I left the hotel room and went for a walk to get back into balance. I remember leaning against a tree on a cliff overlooking beautiful Lake Okanagan, and I started to sob uncontrollably. In the midst of this, I heard a gentle voice within say, "Love him." To which, I defensively replied, "I do love him!" But the voice kept patiently repeating, "Love him. Love him." I realized then that I did not love Matthew for who he was, but for who I wanted him to be. That moment changed our relationship forever. More than a decade later, we are the best of friends, great business partners, and we have deep respect and love for each other.

RELEASING THE JUDGE PATTERN

To develop awareness of the Judge within, it's helpful to recognize the words commonly used that activate this power pattern. The Judge often uses a statement or question as a form of judgment. For example, the Judge might say, "Isn't that interesting," yet with no genuine curiosity, just judgment. Some questions might seem innocent enough: "Why did you decide to buy that dress?" "How come you drove there?" "What are you planning to eat?" But with these questions, not only is the Judge ready to assess your response as good or bad, but they are also expressing the Controller power pattern, which indirectly says, "If I don't approve, I am in control."

When you find yourself making comments and asking questions that are designed to feed the Judge and Controller, stop and don't say anything. Smile and simply radiate love to the other person. Within moments, you will feel the difference, and so will they.

7. The Chosen One

This power pattern is common in younger generations whose parents have raised them to be different, unique, and special. At first glance, it seems like a refreshing change from those of us raised with no praise or positive reinforcement. But in this case, the pendulum swings to the extreme, and the power pattern expresses a desire to inhabit the earth as the king or queen—as they were in their parents' homes. The result is entitlement: the world owes the Chosen One for simply existing.

Another term for "Chosen One" is "special." The special energy
shows up in people breaking rules because they are beyond rules—not
because the rules don't make sense or don't serve the mass population.
It shows up in a lack of motivation to make a difference in the lives of
others, apathy, and lack of commitment or follow-through. Specialness
is difficult for people to see and own, because they are strongly
resisting the Law of the Impersonal. The world has revolved around
them for so long that they cannot see other possibilities that can shift
the focus from "I" and "me" to "we" and "us." The special person, or
Chosen One, is often perceived as selfish and vain; underneath it all,
they simply fear not being noticed and seen. They have a belief that
says: "If I'm not seen, then I don't exist." How can they exist if the
universe is impersonal?

The Chosen One also believes in immunity to the laws of time. They
expect things to be instantaneous; they shouldn't have to wait or work
for anything. They perceive their time to be more important than
anyone else's. If the Chosen One does not grow up and out of this
pattern, they often take on the energy of the Blamer and Controller,
demanding that things be their way and only their way. They become
a living nightmare for many an organization or family unit, as others
may find them engaging in threats, aggression, and intimidation to get
their way. This is common when the Chosen One is left to inflate their
power pattern while having no conscious awareness of the behavior
that drives it.

"Special" people often abdicate their responsibility to participate in
the collective good. They don't believe in traditional systems and
institutions, yet they have not found anything to replace what no
longer works. Apathy sets in, and the complainer energy takes hold. As
a group, they tend to be non-committal. Then, when things don't go
well due to their lack of commitment, they blame others for it. They set
up an us vs. them paradigm, creating divisiveness rather than unity.

The Chosen One is particularly drawn to the "special relationship" in intimate partnerships. They believe that there is only one person in the entire universe that is meant to be their soulmate. When they find this person, they idolize them, and fully expect the relationship to last forever, with little or no work involved, because, after all, it was "meant to be." Then when the special person no longer behaves according to the Chosen One's rulebook, they lament, asking, "Why are you doing this to me, God?" They demand a personal answer from an impersonal source of universal love. They cannot see that their former perfect mate is not "the love of their life" but rather, "the lesson of their life." And by not seeing the lessons gifted to them in the relationship, the Chosen One continues to express the power pattern, reinforcing their belief that they are chosen and so must endlessly seek the perfect chosen mate. The Chosen One would do well to practice seeing all beings as special—yet no one as particularly special. They would do well to practice loving for the sake of loving, and not for the sake of reinforcing their own or another's specialness.

RELEASING THE CHOSEN ONE PATTERN

The way to rid yourself of this power pattern is to begin practicing unity consciousness: see all relationships through the eyes of love. See all people equally. When there is no separate love, you will be free to see yourself and others for who they really are: powerful beings with infinite potential.

Begin with observing the words you think and say. Some common phrases of the Chosen One power pattern are:

> *"I'm not going to be a part of that." (…I'm beyond this movement.)*

> *"That idea is lame." (…I judge you because I think I'm better than you.)*

> *"I deserve more." (…because I was born!)*

*"I need to be with different people." (...I don't see value in
connecting with people who cannot rise to my level of significance.)*

When you disengage from these thoughts and begin to develop quality
relationships with genuine connection, where equality on all levels is
honored, lasting influence can occur.

8. The Withdrawer

This is the force that lives off the fear that we are not capable of
influencing our own destiny or contributing to positive change on the
planet. Like the Controller, the Withdrawer buys into the belief that
the earth and its inhabitants cannot be trusted, and that the universe
is not safe. They will choose to be silent at those very times when it is
important that their voices be heard. It will choose to follow, even if
following goes against the grain of who they are. Choice is abdicated to
someone else who is perceived as a leader.

The Withdrawer will also abdicate personal responsibility, which can
lead to complaining and passive-aggressive Controller tendencies.
Even if the Withdrawer doesn't develop these traits, the danger is that
they will be taken off the hook; they'll simply be that "nice and quiet"
person that everyone likes. They will be the person in the background
who never fully radiates pure power, because they've let it slip into
apathy and numbness. While it might not be evident to their social
network, it can have devastating effects on those they are closest to,
and can sometimes result in the severing of long-term relationships.
On David Hawkins' consciousness scale, apathy calibrates at fifty,
with only shame and guilt vibrating lower. Most people who have a
job that they don't like are in this low vibration. Combine that with
a disengaged love relationship and no connection with family and
friends, and you have a recipe for disaster.

Apathy and disengagement eventually define the Withdrawer's behavior. As Brené Brown, author of *Daring Greatly*, discovered in her research, the greatest form of betrayal—beyond marital affairs, businesses that have gone wrong, and family feuds—was the betrayal of disengagement. When disengagement occurs in a marriage or family, the Withdrawer gets defensive and insists that they are, in fact, fulfilling their obligatory roles, so just leave them alone. (Stop nagging.)

The Withdrawer force may lead us to believe that we have the noble quality of being a conscious and dedicated, hard-working person, but the true test of whether we are in our pure power is if we make choices that are for the good of all. In this case, withdrawing from others, disconnecting from our purpose, refraining from expressing truth or ignoring inner guidance, are not actions that are for the good of all. They stem from a core fear that we are not worthy and therefore don't deserve to take our place and space on the planet.

RELEASING THE WITHDRAWAL PATTERN

One way to work through Withdrawal energy is to make a commitment to be a witness each time you lean away from a person, thing, or event. Open your heart and mind to experience the present moment exactly as it is, not forcing, but also not withdrawing. Pay attention to the language you use in conversation.

Withdrawer language often sounds like this:

"You choose." (Abdicating their role.)

"I don't know." (Giving up on their gift of inner wisdom or outer experience.)

"Whatever you want."

"It doesn't really matter." (When it does.)

When at its lowest, the Withdrawer manifests depression, goes into Victim consciousness, and may even have suicidal thoughts. Frequent thoughts are: "I don't belong here, and I just want to go home." When this force makes the choice to commit suicide, people left behind often say, "If only we knew. If only we were told what was really going on." This is typical of Withdrawal energy: lack of communication, lack of connection, and not asking for help. If you are in this energy right now, I urge you to seek assistance. Reach out to a professional who can assist you in coming to terms with your challenges. If you are seeing early signs of withdrawal in yourself, begin to say the opposite of what you've always said and thought, such as, "I choose. I know what's best for me." "Every choice I make matters." "I am home in my heart, my mind, my body, and my spirit." And then follow through on what you choose. In this way, you will begin to have a sense of purpose—that you are here to improve human or planetary conditions and guide others along their journey, because you've been through your own.

Reflections

Take the Power Archetype Quiz found on www.KarenMGregor. com to discover what your power archetype is. You'll gain further understanding of specific light and shadow aspects of your personal power and how you navigate that power.

By being aware of power patterns, celebrating the new awareness, and then choosing to dissolve these patterns in yourself, you become an influencer. After examining all the power patterns, review the last couple of days or weeks and see how each power pattern has played a role in your thoughts and behaviors. Notice how some power patterns are dominant and have become a habit. Others have no grip over you and rarely, if ever, show up.

Not surprisingly, it is easiest to spot power patterns in relationships other than our own. Provided you don't adopt a "holier than thou" attitude, you can start there. Simply observe (without judgment) the power dynamics between two individuals you know well and how the patterns of power work in tandem to wreak havoc. Take your mother and father, for example. Let's say they came from a traditional patriarchal family and never questioned those ways. Your father walks in the door, and he's late for dinner. Your mother doesn't say anything and continues eating her dinner, although she is angry with him for being late. (Withdrawer.) Father asks Mother how her day was. Mother gives him the silent treatment. (Controller.) Father responds by saying, "Well, thanks for asking how my day was," and launches into a monologue that all he ever does is work, and then he's treated so poorly. (Victim.) Mother then says, "Well, since your day is going so badly, it's a good thing I made your favorite dessert." (Savior.)

Take a moment to go inward and consider a relationship that you are struggling with. Notice the power dynamics between the two of you, paying attention to your own power patterns at play. Write them down, and play out a typical scenario, rewriting your part in it. How will you think and act so that you are no longer hooked into these power patterns? Reflection increases awareness, and heightened awareness typically leads to engaging the pure power necessary to be an influencer in the Way of the Tao.

Then, take a few days to carefully observe your own go-to power patterns. Notice when you choose to *react*, rather than *act* from your pure power. What pattern are you employing? Journal about this pattern, and how it shows up. Each evening, take a few minutes to celebrate the awareness of patterns, even if you chose, in the moment, not to stop them. As one day follows the next, notice even the smallest change in patterns and continue to tweak your reactions until they are positive actions. Notice how you relax and release, accepting life as it presents itself.

By committing to integrating these learnings and dissolving these patterns, you will come to know what true, authentic, sustainable power is. In Verse 10, the *Tao Te Ching* invites us to "know this Primal Power that guides without forcing, that serves without seeking, that brings forth and sustains life yet does not own or possess it."

The following chapter highlights ego needs that are present in each power pattern. When we understand these needs, we can more easily dismantle the hold that distorted power has on us. While freedom is possible, without a roadmap to get there, the journey may take a lifetime. The next chapter provides that roadmap.

Three

Releasing the Ten Ego Needs

The Sage has no fixed heart of his own.
Those who look at him see their own hearts.

—Tao Te Ching, Verse 49

Now that you have more insight and a greater understanding of your personal power patterns, you are in a better position to live your life and influence others from a place of pure power. Now it's time to examine what is underneath those patterns—keeping your heart closed and fixated on them—so that you can free yourself to be a more powerful influencer.

As Lao Tzu says in the quote above, the sage has no fixations—no "fixed heart of his own"—no preferences, judgments, or compulsion for things to go a particular way. Yet most of us have many needs that arise to cope with trauma and avoid experiencing discomfort and pain. In particular, there are ten ego needs that play big roles in energizing our power patterns. Once we hold a power pattern long enough, it becomes part of our personality. As a result, we get pulled out of alignment with our love-power and build up distorted power instead.

Understanding these ten ego needs more deeply will help you recognize when you're engaging in them—when they're feeding your power patterns. The ability to see them in action will empower you to respond differently and give you more freedom from the compulsion to engage. They are:

- The need for approval
- The need to be right
- The need to control
- The need to "get" something from someone
- The need to stay safe
- The need for more possessions
- The need for appreciation and recognition
- The need to be liked and loved
- The need for specialness
- The need to protect against criticism

We'll discuss them one at a time.

The Need for Approval

(Power Patterns: Controller, Victim, Savior, Martyr, and Chosen One)

When you desire approval for something you have said or done, you are asking for validation of your worthiness from outside of yourself. The power patterns that seek validation of worth are Victim, Savior, and Martyr. Victims want their stories to be validated; they want to be seen and loved by others. Saviors want their acts of heroism validated, and Martyrs want their acts of support and care to be appreciated. The Chosen Ones seek validation of their uniqueness.

You might think, "Well, the world could be a little more appreciative and acknowledge kind actions more often!" While there's truth to that, keep in mind that seeking validation can distort your power. Pure power doesn't recognize "transactional behavior;" it isn't concerned with getting something back after giving. Transactional behavior is based on the belief that if the external world doesn't recognize your efforts, you're not enough.

Continuously seeking validation is like bringing water to a well that is always drying up. No matter how much validation, praise, awards, or acknowledgment you receive over the years, it will never be enough to rid the mind of what *A Course in Miracles* calls "the tiny mad idea" that we are not enough as we are.

There's another downside to trying to get approval outside of yourself: even when someone does validate and praise you, your ego will seek the opposite. It will set out to prove those people wrong. And it's a very good detective! You might end up with your ego convincing you that you're a fraud or failure, and it will have plenty of proof to back up its claims. Soon, you become full of contradictions: one minute seeking approval, angry if you don't get it, and the next minute telling yourself that you're a failure, you don't deserve what you have, or you don't deserve whatever new opportunities are arising.

Caught in a pattern of seeking approval from others is also problematic because if we believe, consciously or unconsciously, that our worth is determined by those outside of ourselves, then, in turn, we also believe that the merit of others relies on our judgments. We feel compelled to raise some people up—but only those who deserve it for one reason or another. We take on the Judge pattern, where we feel most safe when we are judging what is approval-worthy and what is not. In that pattern, we live in a bubble of protection, filtering our experiences and relationships, keeping everything at bay that doesn't fit our approval list. Getting stuck in living this way constricts your heart and limits your level of openness to life itself. The less open you are, the less alive you feel, and the less influential you become.

The Need to Be Right

(Power Patterns: Controller, Blamer)

This ego need was difficult for me to work through. I didn't even know it existed until a professor challenged me one day in class. "Karen, why do you always have to be right?" he asked me. I was shocked. I didn't think I was trying to force my views on anyone. But as I looked deeper into my behavior, I saw that I would inevitably feel angry, discontent, or irritable if I left a conversation without having the final word—or without having my views resonating as the *right* views. To a Controller, part of needing to be right means someone else has to be wrong. The belief fueled my Blamer pattern, and I began to point fingers.

Trying to control others and needing to be right diminish our power and weaken our ability to influence. They take the life out of creativity and destroy new solutions to old problems before they get to see the light of day. After all, how can anything new come out of an insistence that we already know what to do? Master painter Pablo Picasso said, "I am always doing that which I cannot do in order that I may learn how to do it." Buddhists call it "beginner's mind;" it is wise to be open to the possibility that we just don't know.

I gave a presentation several years ago, and right afterward, I received feedback about my performance from a roomful of coaches. But instead of being grateful and open to the feedback, I ran it through a filter to determine whether the feedback proved me right about my perception of my talk. If I thought that a part of the talk needed improvement, then I was open to the feedback; if not, I was defensive and closed to it. The coaches became more and more silent. When I watched myself on video later that night and saw clearly how I reacted to the feedback, I decided I would never again shut down to honest feedback just to be right.

> *To know yet to think that one does not*
> *know is best. Not to know yet to think that*
> *one knows will lead to difficulty.*
>
> **—Tao Te Ching, Verse 71 (Translator D.C. Lau)**

Many of us recognize on a gut level when we're defending our ego's need to be right. We know we're being stubborn and ornery, but we still can't help it. It feels out of our control. We want to rid ourselves of the behavior, but we don't know how. Recognizing where it comes from and how it develops can be helpful. Ask yourself: When did I first take on the belief that I was not okay? Or that there is something wrong or bad about me?

My own suspicion that I wasn't enough—leading to the compulsion to prove that I was right—began as a young child. To protect myself from it, I fed my sense of self-worth by throwing myself into my studies. If I could be smarter than everyone else, I reasoned, I could prove my worth. If I knew more than anyone else, I could claim my stake as a worthwhile person. If I could prove my knowledge and wisdom through more degrees and higher levels of achievement, then all would finally be well.

But all was not well. The more that I proved to myself that I was right about the world and the way it was for others, the more I felt unhappy, unfocused, and angry.

Once I became aware of my mistaken belief, "I'm not enough," I began to notice how it showed up, particularly in my need to be right. One of my spiritual mentors, Loree Cowling, helped me further with one statement and two simple questions:

"When building connections with another person, have an awareness of your individual agenda," she said. "Do you want to be altered by the interaction? Or do you want to alter the other person?"

Her questions invited me to look at how often I want to be right so that the other person changes, rather than being open to being changed myself. Wanting another person to change (in other words, wanting them to be wrong!) meant that I could stay safe. But staying safe wasn't what I wanted most, either. When I did what she recommended, my perspective shifted, which opened my heart and fed my curiosity about being influenced by another. Over time, this simple action led to the dissolving of my need to be right, which resulted in more joy and harmony!

The Need to Control

(Power Patterns: Controller, Blamer, Savior)

When we find ourselves on the receiving end of dominating parents, teachers, bosses, or colleagues, it's common to seek more control over our lives and circumstances. But, when tragic experiences of abuse or neglect at a young age have been in the picture, people can develop a deep fear that they won't have any control in their own lives. It's a fear that tells them that if they don't micromanage or obsess, their life will spin out of control, and they'll be at the mercy of a painful and cruel world. Several of the power patterns hold this fear in particular ways: the Controller is afraid of cruelty and a lack of love; the Blamer is afraid of criticism and attack; and the Savior is afraid of not being seen and acknowledged. With fear at the helm, all of these types abdicate their true power.

Once again, awareness helps to free us from our self-sabotage. When I
was younger, I'd sometimes get angry or obsessive when others didn't
have the same opinion as I did, or when they weren't doing what I
thought they should do. Because of it, I was difficult to be around for
much of my early years. When I finally became aware that letting go
of the need to control was a true sign of healing and happiness, I made
it a priority to be on alert for the Controller in me. I began to do small
things for myself—like having a personal time-out before responding
to a challenging email, making a difficult call, or responding in person
to someone who was unhappy with me. Later, I noticed more subtle
improvements, like having the ability to wait patiently in line instead
of needing to barge in and take control. Or listening to my mom share
about her day instead of trying to control her experience by giving
unsolicited advice.

Another way to reduce the impact of your need to control is to be
aware of your body's desire to close down when something doesn't
go the way you expect or want it to. Your heart or your belly will feel
as though it is tightening or closing. In that moment, become aware
of the sensation and the pain your body wants to express and release.
Without paying much attention to thoughts, be with the pain and
allow it to express. This often takes only a few seconds or minutes, and,
generally, the discomfort passes quickly.

Unfortunately, most of us have been taught to avoid feeling our pain.
Instead, we get hooked into the thoughts that accompany the pain.
Because the thoughts are primarily in place to help keep us safe from
pain, we engage them. But by doing so, the thoughts become our
reality, and we get caught up in controlling ourselves, our lives, and
other people all over again.

There is another option, though—one that has a much better outcome.
You can allow the thoughts to simply pass by without hooking into
them. If you feel an emotion start to rise up, relax your body and
allow yourself to feel that emotion but not hook the mind into making

further meaning of it. This is daily practice. If you are disciplined in doing this, it will lead to great freedom and fulfillment.

For those of us who struggle with the Controller within, giving ourselves the opportunity to feel our feelings helps us to step back and see the damage we're doing to ourselves and to those around us. Thich Nat Hanh said, "You must love in such a way that the person you love feels free." I advocate that all our relationships be like this. At the end of the day, it's helpful to evaluate whether our actions, words, and thoughts are in alignment with this intention.

The Need to Get Something from Someone

(Power Patterns: Controller, Savior, Martyr, Victim)

This is a survival need and stems from the fear that you won't be provided for, that there isn't enough, or that you aren't enough. If you experience this need, it pulls you away from alignment with the Tao. You trust life less and less; life feels like a struggle void of joy. If you're a business owner, it might feel like the business will die if you don't get something from a prospective client. Yet that's a highly unproductive energy to be holding: if you operate with the energy of fear and lack, your potential clients will sense something is off. They might want to work with you, but they won't cement the deal, and they won't be able to articulate why. If your goal is to get something from someone, you won't be able to create meaningful, lasting influence.

Instead, focus on your desire to be of service to others. Hay House bestselling author and speaker Doreen Virtue once shared on stage that when she switched her own thinking from, "What can I get?" to "How may I serve?" her business took off. In the beginning stages of business, it's easy to be focused on the first question. But those who fail in business often do so because they don't shift from fear of lack to love of service.

Underneath the need to get something from someone are particular ideas about how we want them to think, act, and behave. When I was single for several years, others encouraged me to "get that perfect man" by making a list of everything I wanted from a relationship. It seemed like good advice at the time, yet every time I met a guy, I brought with me a mental checklist (and a physical one stuffed in my purse!) of everything I was demanding from him. The more extensive my list became, the more frustrated I was that there couldn't possibly be any man out there for me. "The good ones are taken" was the conventional wisdom. When I finally realized the list was burdened with conditions, I dropped it. Instead, I reevaluated my beliefs about intimacy. I got honest with myself about how they were shaping my private agenda to find "the one." Then, I was able to set them aside and allow myself to simply be with my date. I no longer felt compelled to make something happen. I could simply experience peace and happiness, regardless of who was sitting across from me. Once I was in a state that was genuinely me, peaceful and happy, I attracted people who were also living at that level.

> *If you approach life with force you will*
> *get something; if you approach life with*
> *contentment, you will have everything.*
>
> **—The Tao Te Ching, Verse 33**

I'm convinced that the need to get something from someone has resulted in rampant loneliness in the world. Many people only experience an illusory form of goodwill—one that comes with unspoken expectations—instead of unconditional support, which arises from a desire to be of service. As a result, many are suspicious of others and avoid asking for help. In the US, for example, what percentage of the population actually know their neighbors? In contrast, when I traveled through Italy, Poland, and Peru, I encountered daily outdoor gatherings where people broke bread, listened to one another, and had fun. Time was not invested in cell phones and selfies, but in relationships with people who were genuinely connected to each other.

To be an influencer in the Way of the Tao, consider where you can experience unconditional service and connection. How might you incorporate this Taoist principle?

One who seeks his treasure from the outer world is cut off from his own roots. Without roots he becomes restless; his mind becomes weak.

—The Tao Te Ching, Verse 26

It's ironic that the very thing our egos demand—to get something from outside of ourselves—is what stops us from being truly happy and content. Yet that is the ultimate wisdom of the Tao: to let go of the ego's fear that what we want most in the world can only be found outside of ourselves.

The Need to Stay Safe

(Power Patterns: Controller, Victim, Chosen One)

The need to stay safe confronts many of our beliefs, including those about life after death, God, and the idea of a loving universe. Again, depending on events in childhood and adulthood, the need for safety can vary at different points. Sometimes it can become one's primary reason not to pursue greatness. The fear of change—that something will be taken away or something bad will happen—is commonplace. Yet, it can rob us of the ability to be powerful influencers in the world.

My friend Sheryl Wolowyk works as an executive with the XPRIZE, a non-profit organization that designs and manages competitions to encourage technological development that could benefit humanity. Sheryl says, "If you think of life as a game, are you playing to win or are you playing to not lose?"

If you are going through transitions in your life, but you're not taking the necessary steps to reach your dream, answer the following questions:

- *What is it that I am most afraid of?*
- *What will happen to me if this fear becomes reality?*
- *What will happen next—after the fear becomes reality? (Keep asking and answering this question until you have nothing left to say.)*

I use this set of questions whenever I become aware that I am impeding my own progress on something I really care about. After I answer these questions, I am more calm, confident, and happy to take the next step. After you do this exercise, it's important to define your next step—just one step. As each step is completed, articulate the next one. You won't need to do this with every project you undertake, but use it on the ones that seem so out of reach that you don't know where to start. (And if starting means finding a mentor or a coach to help you know where to start, do that first!) By completing your first step and articulating the next, you will gain the confidence to keep going. The Buddha said that there are two mistakes people make: one is not starting, and the other is not finishing. This exercise will help you do both.

The Need for More Possessions and Money

(Power Patterns: Controller and Blamer. May Fit All Power Patterns)

One of the most difficult needs to master is the need for more possessions, particularly the need for more money. Beliefs about money challenge our faith in others, our trust in ourselves, our level of happiness, belief in a higher power, and our need for safety and peace. In fact, very few people make it through life without distorting the meaning of money. We harbor ideas we've constructed about money based on a variety of hurts and traumas from childhood. Most of us have future aspirations that are fraught with anxiety about money. Freedom from these associations with money comes with letting go of the variety of meanings we've assigned to it. When money has no personal meaning, there's no fear, and the child in us feels free.

When I was in Assisi, Italy, writing portions of this book, I was deeply touched by the story of Saint Francis of Assisi. His wealthy merchant father imprisoned him in a tiny cage at the age of seventeen for stealing his money and giving it to the poor. He withheld food from his son for two weeks and locked him up in their home. Completely baffled by his son's generosity, Francis' father decided it was simply teenage folly, but Francis grew up to become one of the world's most recognized and beloved advocates for the poor and promoter of peace and compassion. Francis understood what his father did not: money is simply one of many tools through which we can answer the question, "How may I serve? How may I help?"

To heal your fears about money, bring awareness to those fears. Each time the topic of money comes up, consciously choose a loving, abundant thought and action over fear. Trust the Divine and know that if you listen to and act on your inner knowing, everything you need will be provided to you.

Begin to free yourself from the need for more money or possessions by asking yourself some questions: When you are presented with opportunities that align with your highest values, do you close down within the safety of the Victim power pattern? Or do you say "Yes" to those opportunities and feel grateful for the opportunity? When you say "Yes" to synchronistic opportunities, you align with the flow of abundance and reduce your addiction to lack. Choose what you want to focus on: the flow of the universe or resistance to it. It's your choice.

The Need for Appreciation and Recognition

(Power Patterns: Victim, Savior, Martyr)

Most people love being appreciated and recognized for their accomplishments. The art of appreciating others, whether at work, at home, or in the community, helps them feel seen and heard and supports them to continue on their path. However, I invite you to consider that when you are living day to day as an influencer, the people you influence want to feel that you're not needy. They'll feel your fullness and clear energy when you're completely present to them in your interactions. If a need to be appreciated or recognized arises, it takes away from our ability to be present. When I was in high school and college, I used to live my life for moments of recognition. Instead of following my passions, I strove to get good marks—just to be recognized.

When we're controlled by the need to be recognized, we've created a series of expectations and laws about the way the world should work and how people ought to behave. Yet the creation of these expectations stems from fear of not being loveable and not being seen as worthy. Expecting others to appreciate us inevitably feeds the ego and can lead to blaming, passive-aggressive control patterns, launching into Victim stories, or stepping into Martyr patterns. To prevent that from happening, release anything you expect to get as a result of good deeds—whether it be from people, from the earth, or from the Divine.

I've heard many people talk about feeling unappreciated and unloved. They share stories about who did what and who said what—while the sharing itself contributes to their suffering and can negatively impact the energy of people around them. If that's you, stop and notice. Make the choice to return to the love-power you were born with.

The Need to Be Liked and Loved

(Power Patterns: Victim, Savior, Martyr)

This need is a little counterintuitive. After all, we all need to be liked and loved, right? What could be wrong with that?

While the need for love can serve us as children—helping us build confidence and appreciate ourselves—influencers cannot thrive when driven by a desire for approval and love from other people. Rather than our supportive actions being unconditional, they become transactional: "I will be of service to you, but somewhere deep inside, I must see that you approve of what I say and do and who I am." The transaction puts us in the position of conditionality—*this* happens only if *that* happens—and reduces our capacity to truly influence.

The need to be liked or loved can also turn into an addiction. Some people go to great lengths to ensure that others don't show them signs of disapproval. They sacrifice who they really are for their perceived relationship to be calm and amicable. They can lose their sense of self, they can violate their own boundaries, and they can resort to completely irrational behaviors that they later regret.

I was one of those people. I was addicted to a relationship that was tumultuous from day one. For several years, we broke up and then got back together many times. This relationship began shortly after my fourteen-year marriage ended. Looking back, I jumped in quickly when I found myself alone for the first time in my adult life. Desperate not to feel loneliness, I was willing to do almost anything to make the partnership work. I loved him deeply, I thought, but I did not love him as described in the Way of the Tao. I thought I was being a "spiritual" being, compassionate and forgiving, but I see now that I only took steps to forgive him out of a fear of being alone and rejected. I also worried about being seen as less-than in the eyes of my family, my community, and ultimately, myself should I have another failed relationship. My fears convinced me I was doing the right thing by acting and thinking in ways that were not in alignment with my deeper truth.

If you find you have the "disease to please," and you are easily hurt by criticism or the opinions and judgments of others, I encourage you to begin training your mind to see that you, and you alone, are giving meaning to what is happening. Ask yourself: What do I make this incident mean about others? About myself? Is it possible that I have created the meaning I give this? Am I willing to let go of the meaning I've given this situation—not to appease or please—but to focus on discovering my true nature?

It's easy to blame others who have not accepted us as we are. It is more difficult to go within and discover who we really are beyond all external illusion, stories, and perceptions.

Man was not made to blow out air—he was
made to sit quietly and find the truth within.

—Tao Te Ching, Verse 5

The Need for "Specialness"

(Power Patterns: Savior, Martyr, Chosen One)

The concept of a "special relationship" originated in *A Course in Miracles*. It states that the ego loves to consider certain people in our lives special, and to be able to consider ourselves special in the eyes of someone else. This is most evident in romantic relationships. We believe there's "the one"—that perfect match for us; someone who finally sees us for who we really are. Having this belief, we are compelled to go hunt for that unique person who will consider us special. But it's a chase that's based on an illusion.

Gabrielle Bernstein, author of *Spirit Junkie*, says it beautifully: "Whenever you make someone special, you separate yourself from the opportunity to learn true, connected love. You forget that we are all one."

The truth is that the people we meet are here to help us grow in love. It's not complicated; it's beautiful in its simplicity. Once you accept this perspective, then hundreds, if not thousands, of people could be that to you. They are all "the one." They can help you grow to be more loving, more compassionate, and more in your pure power. And "help" does not mean that they are a savior or mentor to you. In fact, they might even challenge you and present obstacles to your ability to fulfill your soul's mission to love unconditionally. Indeed, your "soul mate" could be the one that triggers old wounds and makes it more challenging to love.

I love romance, but I've come to believe that it's usually founded on the need to be special. In their quest for romance, people often crave attention and are only momentarily satisfied that they are indeed someone's "somebody." The ego's desire for belonging, to be enough, and to be seen, has been met.

Searching for "the one" can lead to a prison of one's own making. I've seen people locked in this prison their entire lives, never escaping the constant craving for specialness. At the same time, they often deem another special as long as they behave according to their personal Rule Book. Love is evident from many behaviors and traits, but specialness is not one of them. Never confuse love with specialness. Love supports a life of joy and love-power; "specialness" impedes it.

Specialness can inhibit professional relationships as well. For example, do you treat those "beneath" you or "above" you in your organization differently than others? Influence dissolves when the mind's perceptions are not aligned with love and equality for all. Corporations would do well to emulate the metaphor of King Arthur's Roundtable, which aspired for all to be treated equally. When no one is special, and no one is controlling another, true internal leadership and creativity take place.

When you carve out special relationships at work, you've implicitly designated other colleagues as *not* special—perhaps considering them contentious, difficult, or irritating. For organizations as a whole, the need for specialness can inhibit their forward movement. Suspicion can grow as people learn to feel safe with only a small number of people, missing the opportunity to connect with others in the organization.

But what about those who are difficult to love? Loving someone who is easy to love is easy. But what about those you have little patience with? How can you love such a difficult person? Your first step is to try to understand the person. Try to perceive them without judgment. Ask questions and be open to their answers. Try to accept the person exactly as they are, with no desire to change them. You can remind yourself, "I choose to see this person as equal. I choose to see their Divine potential." Then, get to know them more deeply. Get a sense of what their purpose is and then love, support, and serve them, using your newfound understanding and acceptance. If they seek your guidance, offer it with an open heart, rather than a desire to change them.

Keep in mind that some people aren't ready for support and will reject it. You can still love them anyway and continue to support their growth while not being attached to a particular outcome.

The Need to Protect Against Criticism

(Power Patterns: Controller, Blamer, Chosen One, Judge)

Having grown up German Catholic, I like to joke with my audiences that I believed I was "perfectly guilty." In the drive to be my best and do my best, I developed an aversion to criticism—or what I perceived to be criticism—so much that I wouldn't read the feedback of clients or my audiences. If I had one critical review and ninety-nine excellent ones, I'd be crushed, and I'd stew on it for days.

But receiving feedback and applying what is useful is not only important, but necessary to those who want to be influencers. When I first started presenting talks and workshops, one of my biggest regrets was that I didn't ask for more qualified feedback from people who knew the industry and were familiar with my topics. It would have put me lightyears ahead and helped me influence thousands more people.

Feedback shouldn't be feared. Powerful people embrace it. Ray Dahlio, founder of Bridgewater Associates, L.P., a leading investment company, creates an environment at work where it's safe to offer dissenting opinions. Each employee is not just invited, but expected, to challenge and critique at every level of the company. Imagine being in a culture where it is normal to give and receive helpful feedback! Imagine how much more influence we could have on the planet if we all could embrace feedback this way!

In a similar way, Steve Jobs gave an annual award to an Apple employee who would challenge him in a way that led to company growth and product perfection. Sheryl Sandberg, COO of Facebook, says she is constantly asking for feedback from employees she is connected to. She notes that she genuinely cares what they think and what their concerns are, and this creates a culture of safety. Influence happens when people feel safe to critique as well as learn from their mentors and bosses.

I encourage all leaders to create a culture of challenge in their personal and professional lives. Commit to regularly meeting with a handful of brave people who challenge you just as you challenge them. These are not people-pleasing friends; they should be qualified to critique and have dissenting opinions. Dr. Norman Vincent Peale said, "The trouble with most of us is that we would rather be ruined by praise than saved by criticism." Be open to loving criticism and challenging questions.

It may seem counterintuitive, but to help you deal with being on the receiving end of criticism, explore where you yourself blame, judge, or offer unsolicited advice. Every great leader with lasting influence minimizes blame and focuses on personal responsibility instead. Both Sheryl Sandberg and Ray Dahlio, for example, talk openly with their teams and audiences about their own shortcomings and acknowledge their personal mistakes. In turn, they encourage others to do the same. The magic in doing so is that, over time, one learns to distinguish between one's ego projections and the helpful support of colleagues. We discover that our reaction to others is opinion—not truth.

***

While it's clearly not in our best interest to hold onto the ten needs, most of us do so every day. Although it may seem hopeless at times that our minds have such absolute control, there is a way out. Patience with training the mind is central to cultivating a state of influence. Daily practice is necessary to begin the process of returning to our true power.

Reflections

Carry a list of the Ten Needs with you as you go about your day. Keep them in a place where you can look at them often, such as a small notebook or on an app on your phone. Place a checkmark next to the needs that arise throughout the day. It's an awareness exercise: you might notice some thoughts trying to convince you that the need is real, or you might become aware of the action or reaction you experience when fulfilling one of the needs. Notice which needs show up numerous times and which power patterns they feed.

Commit to addressing one of your dominant needs per week. Take a few minutes every day to close your eyes and ask your body or inner child, "What do you require of me to assure you that I no longer access this need?" Then listen. You will be clearly told. Assure your body or inner child by responding, "Yes, the wise and mature me will make sure to supply that." If your mind rebels, remind yourself that you can relax and release the thoughts as they come up, without giving them meaning.

Four

Seven Ways to Illuminate Your Power

*The Sage lives in harmony with all below Heaven.
He sees everything as his own self. He loves
everyone as his own child. All people are drawn to
him. Every eye and ear is turned toward him.*

—Tao Te Ching, Verse 49

Now that you have an understanding of the source of true power and have greater recognition of what hinders the expression of it, it's time to learn some methods to help you open up your channel of power. Your goal is to choose love over fear, moment by moment, allowing a pure channel of love-power to express itself for the highest good. This chapter gives you tangible, concrete practices that can help you free your mind from disturbing or distracting thoughts and free your true power to express itself fully.

Like nature, our minds abhor a vacuum. When we acknowledge and release destructive power patterns and ego-centric needs as described in the previous two chapters, the mind panics, because it has no anchor to hold on to. Training the mind to be empty for long periods of time is a noble practice, but it's not feasible in today's fast-paced world. It's also exceedingly difficult for most people; the mind is driven to continually protect us from the suspicion that we are not enough. It chatters non-stop in an effort to direct us away from that primal wound. That's why it's important to have tools and methods to fill the inevitable vacuum with positive patterns and love-based habits.

I have seven go-to methods that I recommend for strengthening your love-power while simultaneously weakening the grip of power patterns and ego needs. For best results, implement one method at a time, making each a part of your daily experience. When one practice becomes second-nature, move on to the next, gradually illuminating your true power. The seven methods are:

- Create a new language
- Choose silence
- Practice gratitude
- Practice acceptance
- Choose humility
- Choose forgiveness
- Experience the power of prayer

Create a New Language

 The first step to help you hone your power is to create your very own dictionary of words to use regularly and to replace old, habitual, fear-based wording. Language is a great place to begin, because working with it not only helps dissolve patterns, it creates a new, empowering way of being.

Words are powerful: they can be used to lift our spirits, or they can drag us down in an instant—and others with us. There are many such words and phrases that minimize our power, but since we're so habituated to using them, we don't recognize the damage they do to us. So, when your mind spins its story about what's wrong with your world over what's right, notice the words used. It will help you awaken to the impact of your words. I've become a sleuth in seeing the power patterns that show up and the accompanying words that feed those patterns.

For example, the word "busy." People with Martyr power patterns often use the word to make sure everyone else knows how much time and effort they are sacrificing for others. Saviors often say it to make sure they are getting acknowledgment for helping to make the world a better place with their fixing and saving. Victims say "busy" to broadcast the time-traps and time-for-money traps they find themselves in. Controllers speak it to ensure that every minute is accounted for and that there is justification for never having space for anything else in business or life.

Even if you don't tend to exhibit some or all these four power patterns, chances are you use the word "busy" or some version of it in ways that distort power. A mentor once told me that she thought her life was "wonderfully full." What a beautiful replacement for the word busy! Daniel Gutierrez, author of *Radical Mindfulness*, tells the story of reaching out to renowned meditation singer, teacher, and author, Michel Pascal, as they were to perform at Carnegie Hall on the same night. Daniel began the conversation by acknowledging that Michel might be too busy to talk. Michel said, "Daniel, my calendar is very busy, but I am never busy." Daniel never forgot his words. They are the words of a person who walks in the Way of the Tao.

Another overused word is "absolutely." The word is often intended to be an expression of enthusiastic agreement with another person. But the word itself can often shut out differing perspectives, open-minded thinking, or lively debate. It can be a quick way to dismiss someone who might want to share some of their deepest concerns or values.

Instead of using the word "absolutely," try stopping to digest the words of another and instead say, "I'm curious about that. What is another perspective you might take?" Consider being curious. Albert Einstein once said that he has no particular talents except being intensely curious. Another replacement for "absolutely" could be the response: "What other possibilities exist?"

Another word that needs replacement is "tired." When I was in my twenties, teaching, a good friend often joked with me, saying that I was predictable, adding that when she asked me, "How are you doing?" I would inevitably respond, "I'm tired." This one phrase helped to create within me a negative mindset, disengagement, apathy, and a sense that life was difficult and overwhelming. Try saying this to yourself ten times! You'll probably end up feeling lower energy or even find yourself yawning! We convince ourselves of our energy states through our words.

After creating a new language, I tell myself something very different than I used to when I felt my energy dropping. I tell myself, "I'm going to have a nap, and when I wake up, I will feel refreshed, energized, and ready to work or play!" I don't try to ignore the sensations of my body—doing so would shut down communication with the body. Rather, I give my body what it needs without creating a dramatic story to go along with it.

Once I realized the power of words and began choosing words like "energized" instead of "tired," I became more curious as to what contributes to the state that I want (vitality) rather than the state that I don't want (exhaustion). Over time, I chose to eat less sugar and cut down on carbs. Then I became vegan to assist my body's digestion, and that, combined with less carbs, skyrocketed my energy. I began to forget what that never-ending cycle of exhaustion felt like, because my vocabulary became my action—which became my reality.

When I was in my late twenties, on a return flight from a vacation in
Jamaica, a flight attendant asked me what I did for a living. I told her
that I was a teacher, and she asked, "How do you like it?"

I told her, "It's all right. But kids nowadays don't want to read.
So, it's tough." I was expecting sympathy—but what I got was my
greatest lesson.

She asked, "So what are you going to do about it?" I was shocked
speechless. I had developed a comfortable habit of saying some
combination of "can't," "won't," and "shouldn't." I had never
before been challenged to move from my helpless vocabulary to an
empowered vocabulary—from victimhood to empowered action.

Sometimes words appear to have a positive intention, but upon closer
examination, many hold an undertone of a power pattern at work. One
such word is "deserve." For example, when someone shares a recent
achievement of some sort, a common response is, "Good for you. You
deserved that." But the word is based in the binary of good vs. bad and
is in frequent use by those with a Judge power pattern. If that's you,
you might judge that some people deserve what they receive (good or
bad), and some people do not deserve what they receive (good or bad).
This leads to a resistance to the Law of the Impersonal. If a friend gets
cancer, you might think, "She doesn't deserve that." But who does?

When we use Judge words like "deserve," we tend to resist accepting
things as they are. We believe that we prove our worthiness if we
perform according to our Rule Book—as should everyone else. If
others behave in certain ways, we consider them worthy. They deserve
what they get (all the good), or they deserve what they managed to
avoid (all the bad).

Another word I recommend eliminating—and one that almost
everyone uses—is "but." When someone asks you how your day is
going, do you say, "It's okay, but…"? Do you start to share a story

of excitement or appreciation and then end with "but…"? If you genuinely feel the need to share a negative thought or emotion with someone, do it sparingly. Not only are you taking yourself down and out, but energetically you are doing the same for the people listening to you.

Complaining also shows up in phrases like, "If only…" "Remember when…?" and "what can we do?" The more you use complaining language, the more you keep your power patterns alive, especially the Victim and the Martyr patterns. Challenge yourself to go seven days without uttering one complaint. After managing that, go two more days without engaging in complaining thoughts. Note that you may be disappointed with your attempts, and self-judgment might come up, but see it as just another power pattern that is trying to keep you from elevating your love-power. Laugh at the Judge within yourself and remind yourself that this journey is not hopeless. It is hope-filled when you take daily steps to dissolve your power patterns.

Choose Silence

 A second step to hone your power is to learn to say nothing during conversations that don't necessitate speaking up. Some discussions require our voice to be heard for the benefit of all. However, in the chatter of everyday conversation, learn to become quiet within a sea of noise; it will help you recognize when truth shows up. People share their version of the truth, but these are not eternal, unchanging Truths. They are simply personal truths driven by a cocktail of fears. Lao Tzu knew this well, and warned others, "He who knows, does not speak. He who speaks, does not know."

If we choose to speak every time a conversation takes place, we are more likely to react rather than receive. We are less likely to be able to recognize people's fears and the way they express fear. Learn to stay quiet and get curious about what drives people to talk and act as they do, rather than getting drawn into their words and opinions. The more you can witness the illusion that others live with, the more compassion you will develop for them. Lao Tzu invested a lifetime teaching three things: simplicity, patience, and compassion. Being silent is one doorway to all three of these qualities. Sacred texts around the globe illustrate the same theme, including this well-known Bible verse:

A time to tear and a time to mend, a time to be silent and a time to speak.

—Ecclesiastes 3:7 NIV

When you're drawn to share wisdom, or when someone asks you to share, you may naturally have words, but they are few, and they land deep. People often have profound respect for those who share insights without the noise of excess words. Stay quiet in your response. The fewer the words, the greater the wisdom. The ego desperately wants to take over and talk endlessly, but authentic power within will never guide you to say more than what is necessary to reveal truth.

Using few words with great wisdom is precisely what intuition offers. Divine Guidance may come as a feeling, an image, or an inner voice. How do you tell the difference between Divine Guidance and the ego chattering away? One of the best clues is that Guidance usually uses few words. It is direct, concise, and often, directive in its support. "Do this." "Go there." Do that." Lots of simple, powerful verbs. "Love him." "Call your mom." "Don't sign that contract." "Rest." Still, many of us get caught up in fantasies of what our Guidance is telling us, with long, drawn-out conversations and elaborate details. That is most likely fantasy, not Divine Direction.

Choosing words carefully and with intention results in a communication pattern that mimics Divine Guidance. In other words, the power that emanates from your soul has a language it shares with you daily. When you match that language with an outward expression of conversation and thoughts, you are in pure love-power. You walk the Way of the Tao and become a true influencer.

Practice Gratitude

 A great place to start increasing your gratitude is to journal about all the things you are grateful for. Doing so opens the door to seeing just how abundant your life really is. Choose words that reflect your gratitude and develop a more expansive vocabulary around it.

If you journal daily, you might tend to settle into a habit of mindlessly using the same words and writing a checklist without really *feeling* the state of gratitude. Try to avoid that. It can do damage to your power and distort it by creating an illusion of gratitude that is actually borderline apathy. The true power behind gratitude is our love-power, and so we must *feel* what we are grateful for. For example, there has been loud construction behind my home every morning for the last year. While three neighbors moved away because of the noise, I was able to transform it into my morning alarm. When I hear it now, I feel grateful for starting a new day, and I feel excitement and appreciation for waking up in a comfortable bed without having to set an alarm. After all, I have one just outside my bedroom every morning!

Now I wake up and hear the birds' glorious singing beyond the construction, and I am so appreciative that these birds choose to make a pit stop nearby to share their songs with me. While some of my neighbors felt like victims fleeing their homes, I feel blessed. While both versions of reality are "true" for the individuals experiencing it, which one would you like to wake up to each morning? You can make that choice.

Brian Smith, founder of the American footwear company UGG, says that in the first few years of his marriage, when he and his wife lived in a small apartment with thin walls, she got annoyed from the sound of kids playing ping pong late into the evening. He'd respond by saying, "Wow. I bet it would be great fun to join them!" He shifted his perspective from negative to positive. He adds, "I enjoy the quiet more than anything else. But the environment you are in is what you have to deal with. It's not good or bad, it's the noise of life, and sometimes it's a beautiful thing to listen to it. It's fun to think of it in those terms."

When experiencing conflict within or without, focusing on gratitude can help to supplant old power patterns you've relied on for years and years. If you are angry with someone or arguing endlessly, remove yourself and ask, "What is the gift in this moment?" Without blaming or shaming anyone, feel into your heart and ask, "What am I grateful for?" Dr. John Demartini says that forgiveness can be a statement of gratitude, as in: "Thank you *for giving* me this experience." When we are consciously aware of the gift in our experience, we can more readily drop old power patterns and enter a state of openness to the opportunity the moment presents. Reflecting on the most challenging people and events in your life, can you see the gift in appreciating them all equally? Can you see even one positive trait or perspective gained because of this encounter? This is a form of gratitude: to be able to see the good that is present in every situation.

From my many years of operating businesses, I've developed a very different perspective about what challenges me. I used to want to blame and point fingers at anyone I thought was unreasonable or difficult. Now I'm open to their perspective, and I follow it up by noticing how I can serve people better because of my new insights. Each time there is a challenge, my company gets stronger. If you have a business, you will know that your gratitude for challenge is critical to growth. Without challenges, most companies wither away. Without challenges, most people become comfortable with the status quo and lose the creativity and life force to build something better.

Make it an everyday practice to see how you can improve by noting the challenges and the gifts present in opportunity. Remember to give thanks when you become a better version of you, noting your capacity to handle challenges with love and grace, for the good of all.

Another way to feel gratitude is to sing and dance. Try either activity, and you may just find yourself filled with appreciation and joy! If you feel a sense of withdrawal at the thought of moving your body or using your voice, remember that the idea that you "don't dance" or "don't sing" is just a thought you made up to protect yourself from being seen and heard, and to protect yourself from judgment and humiliation. In his book, *Mastery of Love*, Don Miguel Ruiz says that shyness is simply the fear of expressing yourself. "You may believe you don't know how to dance or how to sing, but this is just repression of the normal human instinct to express love," he says. I was one of those people who refused to sing, and now that I've been singing every day and even singing in public, I feel the fullest expression of who I am returning. I've learned that Ruiz speaks Truth: the love-power that we all have is naturally expressed in singing and body movement. That is why little children do both—they have not developed the filters and fear that they may be judged.

When we make it a habit to feel gratitude, our inner life shifts. We feel more conscious, more loving, more in balance with ourselves as spiritual beings having human experiences. When I focus on gratitude, I naturally begin to release power patterns because their corresponding emotions no longer have a grip on me. One of my favorite writers and activists, Anne Lamott, writes, "The movement of grace toward gratitude brings us from the package of self-obsessed madness to a spiritual awakening. Gratitude is peace."

Practice Acceptance

 Acceptance is not just a concept; it is an energy felt by opening the heart to love. Resistance is the opposite: closing the heart through fear.

When you commit to repeatedly opening your heart and feeling the movement from resistance to acceptance, you can experience a tangible sense of relief, one that grows as you open more and more.

For years, I resisted the sage wisdom of practicing acceptance, because I was afraid that if I accepted situations, I would not get my way. (Yes, my power pattern was the Controller!) Yet acceptance of what is has nothing to do with one person winning and another losing; it is the Way of the Tao, which is for the good of all. Acceptance doesn't mean giving up when you need to do the right thing. Acceptance includes the ability to put your ego aside to acknowledge the facts of the situation, acknowledge how you are feeling, and give yourself the space to feel and act out of love, instead of reacting to protect old wounds from surfacing. The more you allow emotion to have its space—realizing that it is not meant to stay, but to just have its moment in our body—the more you can manage the situation at hand and move forward in a state of love.

Growth stops when we don't accept what is—we end up embodying the power patterns of the Victim and the Blamer and stay stuck there. Or we become a Controller to ensure that nothing bad ever happens again. Not the greatest strategy!

Accepting responsibility is another aspect of acceptance. By choosing to take 100 percent responsibility for our lives, choices, and actions, we gain the advantage of being able to accept what is and become willing to learn from difficult situations when they arise. Taking responsibility allows us to find out what mistakes can teach us and how they can help us grow.

I've always had a hard time accepting when someone takes something that is not theirs to take. For example, my Rule Book once stated, "Thou Shalt Not Betray Me or Others by Taking Something You Don't Own." Now, I'm not saying that the behavior is okay, but I am now more accepting when things like this happen to me or others. I now take on a perspective that I believe empowers: I take responsibility for my part in whatever happened.

I remember one of my spiritual mentors, Carolyn Myss, telling her audience that she was livid when a contractor stole fifty thousand dollars—promising her a kitchen which was never built. Yet over time, she realized that she needed to take responsibility for her own role in the matter, by being so quick to hand over money without due diligence, contractual agreements and a gradual payment policy for consumer protection. She saw her own role in allowing something to be taken from her and questioned her own actions. That kind of personal responsibility involves full acceptance of a situation.

What about traumatic or difficult childhoods? How do we "accept" those? I believe that adulthood brings with it the opportunity to accept that the past is the past; doing so helps to prevent the past from determining your future. Imagine the freedom that comes from fully accepting the people and events of your past. It doesn't mean that you have to agree with their behavior, only that you're accepting rather than resisting what happened. Imagine the freedom in taking responsibility that way. Imagine never again blaming parents or grandparents or teachers—or anyone else who hurt or betrayed you.

Don't despise the conditions of your birth... In
this way, you will never weary of this world.

—Tao Te Ching Verse 72

Not "despising the conditions of your birth" is what it means to be free. It is what it means to be an influencer…to no longer hook into power patterns and waste energy on stories and hurts; rather, to radiate love-power and fulfill your purpose.

Sometimes resistance isn't expressed as pushing something away, but as clinging to it out of a fear that it will leave. This, again, is the opposite of acceptance. The signature trait of acceptance is complete freedom. Clinging defies attachment, closes your heart, and makes others feel less than free. Those who cling are typically desperate for a semblance of control but find themselves out of control and lacking personal peace and fulfillment.

Choose Forgiveness

 Forgiveness will also help you hone your power. Forgiveness is an act of love for yourself, as well as compassion for another, and leads us to give our gifts in service to others and the planet. People with lasting impact on the world have made the decision to forgive and to use the gifts that originated from their wounds—rather than letting the wound destroy them or distort their love-power. Gandhi, Martin Luther King, and Malala Yousef are great examples of people who have mastered forgiveness to create great influence in the world. By forgiving, we elevate our true power for the good of all.

Most people find it difficult, if not impossible, to forgive what they perceive as serious transgressions. Entire books are written on how to forgive; the Way of the Tao is the way of compassion and forgiveness.

You can start practicing forgiveness by doing three things. First, come to terms with the laws of nature. If you accept the Law of the Impersonal, you won't take the actions of others as a personal affront. You won't dwell on a question like, "Why did they do this to me?" You won't need to ask, "Why did this have to happen?" Second, observe your power patterns. Which patterns have a grip on you and make it difficult to forgive? If you can see the Controller, the Blamer, or the Judge in your thoughts and actions, you can address these patterns to make forgiveness a part of life. For example, if you constantly judge yourself, you also will judge everyone else, and by judging, you cannot forgive yourself or anyone else.

Third, look at your needs. If you need to be right, need to be liked, or need to be special, you'll find it difficult to forgive. Most people are not going to meet your needs consistently, if at all, and so patterns of bitterness and resentment take over. Forgive, and they will lose their grip.

Forgiveness is a life-enhancing act, whereas resistance can steal your vibrancy from you. Many people go to their grave with illness and disease, never having forgiven someone. By doing so, they have forfeited positive influence, since it cannot be sustained in the low vibration of anger and resentment.

Choose Humility

 Humility is central to the *Tao Te Ching*, which holds the perspective that all things are equal. No life form and no person is greater or less than anything or

anyone else. Humility is choosing to avoid identifying with power
patterns or the ego's attachment to success, finances, or belongings.
It is letting go of any of the ten ego needs, especially the need to be in
control, the need to be right, and the need to be special. When letting
go of these needs, we can practice humility by holding others in the
same esteem as ourselves. Practice treating everyone equally—with love
and compassion. See them as brilliant and capable. It may be a different
sort of brilliance, yet seeing each individual's gifts, even when they are
not demonstrating these gifts in the moment, is key to humility.

After centuries of making some headway in the evolution of
consciousness, our world still functions on the unspoken premise that
some people are better than others. Jesus, for example, consistently
defied this belief in words and actions. Many people confronted him
repeatedly as he chose to connect with poor people, prostitutes, and
tax collectors—all deemed unworthy of grace. Jesus demonstrated
compassion through humility. This is true influence.

Satyen Raja, founder of WarriorSage, a leadership mentoring and
consulting company, speaks about inviting people from all walks
of life to gather in community. While he loves his corporate clients
and world influencers, he also equally loves those who are lost,
broken, poor, and suffering mental or physical challenges, and he
welcomes them to his gatherings. This is the way of someone who has
relinquished power patterns in favor of humility. As the Tao says, it
is only with humility that we can move people to action. Love-power
cannot do its job in a mindset of hierarchy and separateness.

Superfoods and raw food guru, David Wolfe, has a similar approach
to creating a community where everyone is welcome. David is often
asked how to build community. What he shared with me brought tears
to my eyes. He said,

> The most important thing is that you have to love people. You have
> people all over the place; loving beautiful people who don't know
> how to take care of themselves, people who are nit-picking over
> everything—you have people who are the healthiest and disciplined
> with their diet but they're mean—and you have to love all of that. If
> you want to be an influencer—you've got to love people, in all aspects.
> You've got to get over yourself—the hot buttons: 'This person is
> irritating' ...we create it all. It's about opening yourself up to love. If you
> want to influence everyone in the world, it's a matter of how far are you
> going to open your heart.

As you open, you can replace power patterns with acts of humility.
If you once saw someone as being below your level in intelligence,
abundance, or spirituality, you can ask your heart to fully see them,
allowing your mind to quiet so that you can experience them in the
light of love. Indeed, these actions are often the only thing that matters
to another—the depth of your care, your open heart of humility.

Experience the Power of Prayer

The seventh way to illuminate your power is to pray.
Prayer is your direct conversation with God; it is your
relationship to love, expressed in words. Prayer is
profoundly sacred and intimate, and it does not come
with a user manual!

Many of us have been taught that prayer is reciting a well-known verse
daily or engaging in a Santa Claus-style petition to get something we
want. Ironically, these actions can lead to disassociation with our pure
love-power.

Let's look more closely at prayer. Why do we ask for things through
prayer? Sometimes, people pray out of concern for loved ones and
sometimes to seek support to evolve to the next level of kindness and

love. But mostly, when we ask-through-prayer, we are trying to satisfy our need for safety. Unfortunately, that kind of prayer feeds insecurity instead of reducing it. Most of us ask for things we hope will lead to personal safety, comfort, and stability of personality or identity. By asking, we continue to feed the insecurity of not knowing.

But what if we could immerse ourselves in the knowingness of not knowing. That is the secret, isn't it? So many of us beg and plead to know why things happen or what will happen if we do this or don't do that. What if the asking is designed to feed the small self, so we never have to stand in our big Self: the all-knowing Self, the one that brings us to the edge of humanity to see through the lens of divinity? Surrendering to and completely knowing that "not knowing" is the answer.

Asking, bargaining, petitioning, and engaging in transactions with the Divine has left so many lost in an empty, one-sided relationship with the Divine. Because the mind demands that any void be filled, many recently turned to what they saw as the next available source of an answer: The Law of Attraction and the science behind getting what we want. The topic was very popular for over a decade and has continued to have devoted followers. Still, we have a yearning for a real, solid relationship with that from which we came. People began expressing more and more that they just wanted to go home to God. They didn't know how to be home with God while living on earth.

To better understand the power of prayer, I journeyed to the Poor Clare's Monastery in Duncan, British Columbia. The beautiful nuns had given up everything they owned to live a solitary life of contemplative prayer. Their primary action for the entire day was prayer. Naturally, I was fascinated to see what they would say about prayer, since they do it all day long!

What they shared with me changed the very foundation of my inner world. They said that prayer is many things. It can be a meditative walk in nature—being fully present to one's surroundings. Prayer can be picking up a sacred text and randomly opening to a page where your eyes come upon a few lines, meant just for you. Prayer can be a feeling of deep gratitude. It can be a community that chooses a prayer to reflect on. It can be saying one of many names for God. The nuns in Poor Clare's Monastery, for example, each have a strong relationship with Jesus. They repeat his name over and over as a form of prayer, both out loud and silently. All these ways to pray have one thing in common: to illuminate a relationship with the Divine.

To understand prayer more deeply, I've looked to those whose entire lives have been immersed in prayer. Saint Teresa of Avilla often talked about prayer as a relationship: "For prayer is nothing else than being on terms of friendship with God." Whatever word we use to represent the Divine, developing that relationship and strengthening it is the prayer that illuminates authentic power.

It's important to note that while prayer is a form of communication, it does not necessarily need words. Saint Teresa of Avilla said, "Prayer is an act of love; words are not needed." In fact, many people around the world *feel* prayer more than they *think* prayer. I grew up in an Indigenous community with most residents being from the Cree Nation. For the Cree, prayer was less talk and more feeling. I remember seeing bright, shining faces looking up to the sky, and the wind blowing in their hair as they prayed. The beauty of it remains with me to this day.

Emotions connected to joy, gratitude, appreciation, wonder, awe, and love can transform us from the inside out. When you emanate these feelings, you radiate your power to influence.

If you are not feeling confident with starting a prayer practice with words, feeling it is a great way to begin. While taking a walk, fill your body with an appreciation for nature and gratitude for your moving body and the air, sun, wind, or rain that surrounds you. When you are with a loved one, stop and be silent. Feel the joy of being in the presence of this person you were gifted to be with. Or create a vision board and spend time every day feeling your infinite potential, your God-power, and gratitude for all that you bring to life and all that it brings to you. If you do want to begin connecting with the Divine through words, begin with a phrase like "Thank you."

One of my friends has a terminal illness. As we sat together one day, I asked her what insights she'd gained from her journey. She quickly replied, "I've learned to say 'thank you' for everything in my life. It is the most powerful prayer."

Her response reminds me of Anne Lamott's book, *Help, Thanks, Wow: The Three Essential Prayers*. In its pages, Lamott explores with humor and sincerity her personal struggles and observations of prayer. She writes that a simple and heartfelt "thank you" opens up a whole new world, and the ability to see the gift in everything (and everyone) that life presents is truly a moment of grace. Lamott reminds us that "thank you" can be more than a personal moment of connection with the Divine: it is good for others, too. "You breathe in gratitude, and you breathe it out, too. Once you learn how to do that, then you can bear someone who is unbearable." Ah, that moment of grace is indeed a miracle, and it is made easier with a "thank you."

There are also powerful short prayers that I like to call, "for the good of all" prayers. One of my go-to prayers of this type is from *A Course in Miracles*:

Where would you have me go? What would you have me do? What would you have me say? And to whom?

—A Course in Miracles, Lesson 71

This set of questions helps us take the focus off power patterns, the need to give up control, and the ego's sense of ownership and responsibility, and allows us to come to the Sacred Table with nothing but a humble willingness to be guided. When you open yourself to be a change-agent and walk the Way of the Tao, questions like these break open your soul purpose and present you with life-transforming challenges.

One of the nuns at the Poor Clare Monastery shared with me that prayer changes the person who's praying from within. Reverend Samuel Shoemaker, a highly respected twentieth century preacher, echoes this thought. "Prayer may not change things for you," he said, "but it changes you for things." I love both sentiments because, as we illuminate our power, we come to see that our ability to have a positive impact on the earth is dramatically heightened. We come to a humble agreement that we are, at least in part, given this life in order to be an agent of change and support the planet. This is true leadership, and it speaks to the heart of the Tao of influence.

When we focus our attention on daily prayer, we reduce the urge to engage in power patterns. We begin to see all of our power patterns as the "grand illusion" that the Buddha spoke of. This is true freedom: to leave behind power patterns and no longer be controlled by them. We experience more joy and more fulfillment as we live life in our love-power.

Reflections

Choose to implement one or two methods of illuminating your power each week. Notice how you feel, how you behave, and how you connect to others as you adopt each method. Notice the quality of your thoughts. Record your insights and celebrations as well as frustrations. Although self-awareness can be grueling at times, the only way to truly advance your consciousness is by choosing to do the work that frees you to be in your authentic power.

Pillar II

Presence

Five

Awakening Presence

"Thirty spokes of a wheel all join at a common hub, yet only the hole at the center allows the wheel to spin."

—Tao Te Ching, Verse 11

It took decades for me to be able to even come close to a state that could be considered "present." I was perpetually trying to control the future by being a workaholic. If I wasn't working, I felt an uneasy, sick-to-my-stomach feeling that I should be doing more. Moments with family and friends were obscured by to-do lists in my head. I remember a time when my eldest son was three years old, sobbing and tugging at my pant leg. I asked him what was wrong. He said, "Mommy, you never listen to me." He had been repeating the same question over and over, and I had been so focused on my next steps for my business that I literally did not hear him. Immersed in fear about the future, I let my Controller power pattern take over. I was focused exclusively on my concerns about how I might get ahead in life and prevent anything bad from happening.

When I started my spiritual journey shortly after my second child was born, I began to look at myself as though I was in a movie. (This is a helpful suggestion for those who have difficulty gaining self-awareness.) I looked at myself from the outside, watching this young mother and career woman's thoughts and actions. What I saw frightened me—yet it was exactly what I needed to see. By placing myself in a movie, I had much greater awareness of how I was interacting with life, with people, and with the events that presented themselves to me. Did I really live my life this way? Was I really so removed from others and from life itself? Yes. My eyes were opened, and I was determined to make changes.

My initial attempts to change were short-lived, mostly because I didn't know what was driving my behavior. I kept imploring myself to "Come back!" from whatever worry or challenge I was obsessing over at the time. I felt mentally unstable and began self-labeling, telling people I had a condition that stopped me from being present. I had no idea that it all stemmed from my younger years when I was highly sensitive, and I didn't feel safe in the midst of the numerous arguments about money and unstable careers that were being thrown about my home life. Subconsciously, I decided that I would do whatever it took to create an environment of safety in my own world when it came to work and providing for my family.

My paradigm of the universe was that it was not a friendly, safe place, so I made sure that I was highly independent. I developed the belief that I must go it alone and do things myself. After all, I reasoned, then I would feel safe and in control. It's no surprise I ended up divorced. This traumatic event at the age of forty left me even more determined to be a strong, independent businesswoman, and I pulled away from all forms of support. In addition to being a Controller, I adopted the Blamer power pattern and saw myself as someone who would always be alone, because others only disappoint. I chose to turn away from the gift of real, solid connections with others and the Divine, connections that I needed most to get back to presence. All of this had spiraled out of my understanding of my relationship with the universe.

Unity Consciousness

At that difficult time in my life, I didn't understand deep human
connection, much less unity consciousness. I'd get frustrated when
I'd hear people say, "We are all one." After all, my mind argued, there
is nothing remotely "one" about attempting to connect with people
I have nothing in common with! Being in my Controller and Blamer
patterns, I began to live in a world of accentuated duality, where life
was black and white and people were good or bad. I developed the
Judge power pattern to distance myself from others and feed my need
to be right. But all that changed one night when I had an experience of
Oneness that left me questioning the world of duality and my strongly
held power patterns.

I was going through a divorce at the time, feeling as though I no longer
wanted to be on the planet. Filled with shame that I couldn't make my
marriage work and that my children were suffering as a result, I threw
myself on my bed and sobbed uncontrollably. In that state, I heard a
voice say, "Focus on your heart." For the first time in my life, I saw
with my inner eye the figure of Mother Mary and heard the repeated
instruction: "Focus on your heart." When I put my attention on my
heart, it became warm and then hot like an oven, radiating energy that
filled the entire room. I then went into what some call the "white light"
of a near-death experience, where I felt that neither I, nor anything
around me, existed in isolation. That is, everything was still there, but
it was One. No separation. My mind was no longer in control, and I
was held in an enchanted, timeless experience of pure love and joy.
Somehow, I came out of that experience that day knowing that this
pure love was all that mattered and all that will matter in the future.
That day, I dedicated my life to being a student of love.

My experience of Oneness led me to want more of it! Yet, the next
day, try as I might, I was not taken back to that reality. For the
next few weeks, nothing happened that came even remotely close

to that experience, despite a number of attempts to bring it back. I was frustrated. How could I continue to live in this world of duality and yet know the truth of Oneness? Was this some cruel joke that I would be the victim of for the rest of my life? I felt like a toddler who had been shown a new toy, only to have it snatched away, never to show up again.

Yet the withdrawal taught me so much more than the unlimited access to this tantalizing gift would have. I began to recognize that the Oneness experience was guiding me to be more present to the people and events around me. I was being guided to connect on a deep level with others through my presence, by "being here, now." It was new to me. Throughout the drama of my divorce, I spent less than ten percent of my days in the now. My lack of presence was having an enormous impact on my relationships with my kids—who were craving Mom's attention—and my relationships with my colleagues, who felt I was disconnected from community. It impacted my relationship with my mom, because my mind was always somewhere else whenever we'd speak, making it near impossible to have a quality connection.

The Oneness experience that I so craved needed to begin with reconnecting to others in the present moment.

Then I participated in The Illumination Intensive program, created by Satyen Raja of WarriorSage. I discovered the "dyad" there, a way to deeply connect with another, first by gazing into their eyes and then by asking a series of questions repeatedly until the Truth was exposed. From this process, many people had a direct experience of the Divine. I already had an experience that was enough to last a lifetime, but the concept of the dyad brought to my attention how very little practice I had in true connection with another human being and seeing them for who they really are. Because I had little practice in being present to another, my relationships were suffering, and my work was less than fulfilling. And even though I was teaching people to enhance their intuitive connection, I avoided connecting with them beyond my teaching role, and consequently robbed myself of true fulfillment and joy.

After the program, little by little, I began to connect more with others, and by doing so, I recognized that we are, indeed, One. I saw that our differences were, in the end, costumes we parade around in. These costumes are a part of our stories, which keep us separate and disconnected from others. I saw how our minds categorize and label others to try to protect us from hurt, keeping unity at bay. Yet when we manage to move beyond labels and categorization, we see great possibilities and become creative influencers.

This is where miracles happen. Miracles occur in the space of unity and presence. When we have the ability and willingness to set aside the mind's desire to judge, assess, and label, the possibilities for positive change are infinite. When we no longer live in the duality of Victim/Savior or good/bad, we're more inclined to live in Oneness. We naturally walk the path of the Tao, and by doing so, influence the world with our ideas and creations.

What Is Presence?

So, let's back up and start with the basics: What is *presence*?

Presence occurs when we immerse ourselves fully in the Holy Moment of Now. It occurs when we surrender our mind's preferences and obsessions and when the body/mind/spirit fills with acceptance and gratitude for everything that crosses our path.

Zen master Thich Nhat Hanh says it this way: "Your true home is in the here and the now." People who experience a sense of home as a state of being have been able to integrate this great truth. People who do not are mired in fear and rarely feel safe being in the moment. Instead, they let their mind take responsibility for keeping them safe.

The problem is, it's an impossible request. The mind might be clever in how it comes up with ways to bandage your fears, but it can never eradicate the root problem—that you believe that you are not safe. If you believe that, you're also believing that you're not okay—and neither is anyone else. To combat these suspicions, you go to work to control your life by avoiding being present at all costs. After all, the most vulnerable place to be in is where there is no past or future and nothing for the mind to hook into as it tries to provide Band-Aid solutions to your anxiety.

We also live in an environment where almost no one is "home"—no one is present. You might be talking to a mind and a body, but often there's no one "there" to connect to. This has become so prevalent that it is accepted as the norm. Many of us hardly expect even our friends, coworkers, wives, or husbands, to be fully present to us—although we still get resentful from the lack of it.

On the other hand, have you ever seen someone enter a room and thought, "Wow, they have a real aura about them!" Or, "I can't take my eyes of this person and I don't know why." The person comes across confident and self-assured; they're almost ethereal. They seem like they are floating around the room, radiating energy. Why? It happens when people have chosen to be present as a way of being; they don't just visit the present moment now and then. While the experience of full presence is rare, our bodies and minds remember it because, energetically, we've come home.

When I interviewed Daniel Gutierrez, the bestselling author of *Radical Mindfulness*, I was reminded of the link between power and presence. He shares:

> When you walk in a room, you know who is powerful in the room—it is the one who is present. It's an energy that exudes from the individual when they are able to stay in the present moment. They are not trying to sell you anything and they are not trying to buy anything. Being

> present is the ability to not play into the future or the past. Presence is
> what you exude as a result.

We seem to know intuitively that we were born with presence and
that it is a close companion of Divine Truth. Not our personal "truth"
consisting of opinions and preferences, but Divine Truth that is eternal
and unchanging. We long to return to that state; that's why we're
drawn to people who demonstrate it. One of the leading spiritual
teachers on the planet, Eckhart Tolle, for example, might not be the
most dynamic speaker in the world, yet auditoriums full of people
hang on his every word—and even his now-famous extended silences.
His presence is palpable. The world is craving presence and desires to
know how to embody it.

Preferences vs. Presence

As humans, we tend to have preferences. We want things to go a
certain way and happen by a certain time, or we hope that certain
outcomes don't happen in the first place. We easily develop passions
for what we like and aversions to what we don't like. Doesn't sound so
bad, right?

But here's the problem with preferences. As soon as we have a
preference for or against something, our mind attaches to it and makes
a written-in-stone rule to either keep that thing or avoid it. The more
we think about our preferences, the more our emotions intensify.
Our need to be right and our need to control kick in. Additionally,
we develop expectations about our preferences being met, whether
they have to do with people, events, or the environment. Expectations
inevitably lead to unhappiness, so they're usually followed by episodes
of blame and victimhood.

Sound familiar?

Most of us have experienced this cycle; some of us are even
addicted to it.

Harboring preferences can perpetuate disappointments of the past and
incite fears of expectations not being met in the future. In other words,
we abandon the present moment and shut down to any experience that
is actually happening *right now*.

A simple example: you or a close friend or family member likely have
a preference on where you want to sit in a restaurant. And if you don't
get that favorite spot, you may be unhappy and look to have more
preferences met so you can make up for the first one not being met.
You ask for the music to be turned down or the heat to be turned up,
or for your food to arrive more quickly or prepared in exceedingly
particular ways. You look to others in the restaurant, judging them for
talking loudly and disrupting your preference for quiet. Those who
are with you begin to feel uncomfortable with your unhappiness and
develop their own preferences involving your behavior!

Yet, hope is not lost. As we run our power patterns and are driven by
the ego needs underlying those patterns, we are still offered a return
to the most precious gift: *presence*. Every time we choose love over
fear, and every time we don't give in to our habitual triggers, we create
space for presence. Life coach Michelle Falcone describes the outcome
of this process as the "clean vessel":

> We all have moments throughout the day that we feel guilty or bad or
> 'Why did I say that?' or 'Why did I forget that?' or 'What did I do?' What
> allows you to be pure and a clean vessel is that in the moment, you
> accept it and surrender to it and let it go. You're not hanging onto it and
> that's what keeps you clean so you can be present.

Daniel Gutierrez also notes that it's not easy to be present, even at
the best of times, as we have about 80,000 thoughts a day. He shares

that we need to have compassion for the very human frailty of getting distracted again and again.

> That's where radical mindfulness comes in, taking a deep breath and redirecting our thoughts on a moment by moment basis, not just once in a while... Sometimes we do have to remind ourselves to take a deep breath, and ask, 'Where am I right now?' And this can be done very quickly. It's work to be aware of our thoughts, but that's where authentic presence comes from, people feel that. The person who is able to authentically be present and be with someone is the one that has the most influence.

Any actions that come from power patterns or ego needs will pull you out of presence. They will launch you into the past or future and keep your vessel full of debris. When thoughts and actions come from your love-power, you are in the present. When you are fully present, it is impossible to distort your power because you are coming from a place of love.

Finding Presence within Conflict

A Sage confronts difficulty but doesn't experience it.

—Tao Te Ching, Verse 63 (Living the
Wisdom of the Tao, Wayne Dyer)

It often seems that, just when we think we're on the road to Oneness, someone shows up (as a gift from the universe) to challenge our commitment to love and unity. They are usually very good at pulling us out of the present moment with their own cocktail of power patterns. They can trigger our power patterns, causing a host of internal emotions. The internal war often leads to external war, and we find ourselves in conflict with the other person.

How do you stop this from happening? How do you return to the peaceful, present moment?

Begin by making the choice to commit to walking the Way of the Tao. Remember that you always have the choice to choose love and act in ways that are for the good of all. Each time we choose wisely, we get closer to existing in a *state* of love, versus a fleeting *feeling* of love. The *Tao Te Ching* reminds us that the sage responds consistently to others, whether or not they are easy to love, because the sage is in a state of love that emanates kindness, compassion, and goodness:

> *Those who are good he treats with goodness*
> *Those who are bad he also treats with goodness*
> *Because the nature of his being is good*
> *Those who are truthful he treats with truth*
> *Those who are not truthful he also treats with truth*
> *Because the nature of his being is truthful.*

—Tao Te Ching, Verse 49

Brian Smith says that in his early years of business he would get really frustrated with people who seemed to be blocking his path to business success. Now, after many years of reflection and self-mastery, Brian has a different perspective on the role these people played in his life:

> They were doing what was in integrity with their own lives. They were trying to live their own lives, make their own decisions, do their own things. I've learned to love those people for giving me a great foil to learn love, forgiveness, and acceptance. It's almost like I want to get to heaven and thank them for coming down and playing the role they did in my life so I can grow.

This perspective is critical to moving forward with the flow of life and recognizing that struggles (showing up in the form of people) are not there to block us, but rather to challenge us to be the best version of ourselves. When we rise to be our greatest self, we become influencers.

Another way to navigate challenges with others is to view them as people living in their own state of illusion. See the fears of the other. See the suffering and unhappiness behind their words and actions. Remind yourself of the Law of the Impersonal—the altercation you're having with another individual is not about you, your worth, or your lovability. It's there to invite you to grow in love and evolve as a conscious human being.

Challenging people are in fact your soulmates—not romantic partners, but people destined to help you grow by presenting you with challenging personality traits and actions you don't like. They challenge you to look beyond your preferences and surrender to what is. They invite you to accept the Law of the Impersonal, while at the same time, saying "Yes" to the opportunity to become a more kind, compassionate, and loving human being.

You can choose to be free of the hold other people have on your happiness and fulfillment. When committing to this choice, you understand that you control your mind, it doesn't control you. The more you choose to disengage from power patterns, the more you empty your mind of stories and illusions, and the more you create stillness. The decision to no longer engage in your patterns is a big commitment. If you really want to be a conscious being, giving your word means something. If there needs to be an official ceremony with others involved, do it. Whatever it takes to no longer engage in power patterns that keep you from true freedom of mind, body, and spirit.

Another skill to help you free yourself when confronted by challenging people is to choose the words we say and think more carefully, as described in Chapter Four. This is more challenging the older we get since many of us have grown up with a vocabulary that creates duality, not unity. We use words to label people, events, and experiences as either good or bad. As soon as we label something, our mind creates an opposite. If we label someone as a rational person, we will judge others to be irrational. If we label someone as smart, we judge others as stupid. When we call someone gifted, we may not see the gifts others bring. Our ego mind is constantly looking to label people, separating "us" from "them." As we release the language of duality and refuse to describe people according to our preferences, we relax and surrender into acceptance without trying to change them or defend ourselves.

We can also disengage with difficult people by recognizing their power patterns and how they come up against our own. Consider reviewing the eight power patterns described in Chapter Two to understand why you attracted someone challenging into your life and what your life lessons are in navigating them. For example, the Victim and the Savior feed each other's insecurities. The Victim needs to be saved to feel worthy, and the Savior needs to feel worthy through the act of saving. After a short while, this relationship pattern turns into a challenging situation because neither the Victim nor the Savior are acting from a place of love; they are using the other to provide relief from the belief that they are not worthy. Both the Victim and the Savior almost always end up resenting and blaming the other, instead of being aware of their individual power patterns and working together to mutually support one another in dissolving the patterns.

Taking ownership of your distorted power patterns is critical to healthy relationships. It starts with you, and your decision to change yourself, without expecting that the other person "should" do what you have committed to. Very often, when you change, the relationship changes. If it doesn't lead to peace for the other person, you can still feel peace because you've released your own distorted power patterns.

Once you make the commitment to use your words wisely and release your power patterns, the next natural step to come back into presence is to create stillness in your life. What you've been exploring up to this point leads to internal stillness. In the next chapter, we'll delve into what you can do to further illuminate internal stillness and experience external stillness. We'll also look at how environmental stillness and organizational stillness impact peace and the ability to be present.

Reflections

As you go about your day, make a small checkmark in your notebook or journal each time you are aware of not being in the Holy Moment of Now. Make a note of what took you out of presence. Reflect on the patterns that emerge. What is most likely to take you out of presence? What thoughts cause you to leave the present moment? Take time twice a day to meditate, releasing these thoughts and allowing your body, mind, and spirit to be in the Now. Record changes in your ability to be present. Note any improvements in your ability to allow and accept what *is* versus fighting it with expectations and preferences. Celebrate each day by reminding yourself that you are on a journey of the Tao that will help you live the Truth of Love.

Six

Sacred Stillness

A still mind can easily hold the truth.

—Tao Te Ching, Verse 64

Learning to be still can bring great gifts; it can strengthen your relationship with the Divine and with the eternal and unchanging Truth. These sacred bonds are nurtured by stillness—it is only the ego that chatters endlessly and creates noise that seems to separate us from Spirit. The voice of the Divine, on the other hand, is naturally still.

As I journey into stillness, I often tune into the voice of the Divine to remind me to become part of the silence and spaciousness. Over the years, I have found three practices that are especially helpful to bring stillness to my internal and external world: meditation, gratitude, and evening reflections. In this chapter, I share the depth and practice of all of them with you.

Meditation

Although I am by no means a meditation guru, there are a couple of things I do that work for me, helping me relax into stillness. First, I find a space that I love and that feels good—a place that's peaceful and abundantly simple. This is helpful because my mind usually looks for things to do, and the simplicity and spaciousness help me be more grounded and relaxed as I begin my meditation.

Then I focus on feeling the universal energy field. When you sit and allow yourself to receive the field within, you will notice that it presents itself as a tangible feeling: a warmth or surge of energy, love, or simply, pure happiness. If you cannot feel it, open yourself to a feeling of gratitude. You can visualize a person, place, or experience that warms your heart and makes you smile. Keep this feeling in your entire body by allowing yourself to receive it. If your mind wanders, don't worry, just come back to the practice of receiving the energy.

Beginning this way puts me into unity consciousness—no separation from anyone or anything—and pure love and gratitude for all of life. I don't have to do anything else to experience stillness. When the body feels the universal flow of love, it wants to stay there, so eventually, this form of meditation won't seem like hard work.

Another powerful tool in meditation is to repeat a mantra. You can use the name of a master of love who walked the earth. Repeating the name or mantra with a gentle focus results in high vibration frequency and keeps your mind from wandering excessively. If the mantra is long, then your mind will want to take over and make meaning of it.

Successful meditation occurs when there is no war between your head and your heart. It's when you are not judging the thoughts that stream endlessly into your consciousness. Allow them simply to ebb and flow without getting emotionally hooked. Surrendering to the experience of thought in meditation is freeing. Loving yourself and having compassion or humor when the thoughts arise brings you to stillness, which is the essence of meditation.

You might find yourself judging other things besides thoughts in your meditation, such as the way that your body feels, the visions you have

or don't have, the feelings in your heart, or the absence of feelings.
This is all part of the process of letting go of your human mind and
body to be able to be present to all that is.

Many times, I've judged the expansive presence I was experiencing
when it seemed to be held only in my body. My mind equated spiritual
connection with everything above me. One day, I heard my Inner
Teacher tell me to descend from the ethers with my energy, but I
resisted the advice. Then I heard a big, hearty laugh, and the voice said,
"God is everywhere." That was enough to remind me that my human
concepts were getting in the way of stillness and connection to the
Divine. I was shocked by my mind's illusion that the higher I went,
the more spiritual and better my meditation was! Now I still enjoy
being in the higher realm and the corresponding sensation, yet at the
same time, I'm filled with joy to be in the space of my heart, on the
earth below me, or to simply feel my hands receiving the calm energy
of meditation. When I let go of my attempt to categorize and judge
the experience of God—the experience of peace and joy—I'm able to
reach stillness.

We live in a world of duality. Good/bad is a dichotomy, and most of
us have bought into it, using it to judge our success and the success
of others. In the world of meditation, we tend to consider thought
"bad," but the truth is that embracing thought is the path to harmony.
Imagine a child trying to get your attention while you're working. You
wouldn't label the child "bad." In the same way, consider that part
of meditation is a loving acknowledgment that thoughts are and will
always be with you.

One of my favorite forms of meditation, Transcendental Meditation,
created and made world-renowned by the Indian guru, Maharishi,
is founded on the premise that thoughts arising in meditation are a
sign of relieving stress. If you don't fight the thought and let it pass by
without giving it any notice, and without intentionally ignoring it, it
serves the function of stress release. If you fight it and enter the good/

bad duality, believing that you "should" be able to have no thought or that your thoughts are frustrating, then you don't get the full benefit of the stillness and peace that meditation gives you. The lesson and practice of letting go are critical to meditation, and if you have the Controller power pattern, it is additionally helpful in dismantling the need to be Supervisor of the universe!

Gratitude

The second practice is gratitude. I no longer "think" gratitude. I simply *feel* it throughout the day. It brings a smile to my face and allows me to be in a happy state of love. Can it be disrupted? Well, I am not an enlightened being…yet…but what I can share with you is that the moments of fear and temptation to reengage in power patterns are reduced because of practicing gratitude. Because of that, I experience more peace and stillness. My mind is not actively thinking of how someone did me wrong or what the next calamity may be. World-renowned author and speaker Tony Robbins, with whom I had the honor of sharing the stage in August of 2018, said something that I repeat every day now: "I tell my mind what to do. My mind does not tell me." Our minds can be trained, and one of the greatest vehicles for training is immersion in gratitude.

Gratitude, like meditation, is closely linked with the practice of letting go. When we're in a relationship, many of us activate the power patterns of Controller, Blamer, or Victim. It can be difficult to get out of it even as we become aware of ourselves acting it out. I believe the way out is to cultivate gratitude for the very practice of letting go. I discovered this as a result of a challenge with relationships. For years, I had expectations of commitment when in relationships yet somehow attracted partners who were non-committal by nature. In response, I'd engage in mental and emotional fixations, which ignited the

Controller, Blamer, and Victim within me. I was constantly resisting the flow of life. Then I began to visualize the relationship in a positive flow and energetically sent love to myself and my partner. I felt deep gratitude for the *practice* of letting go, and I began to heal. Then I realized that letting go, my spiritual goal, was not actually the greatest gift of the experience. It was the *practice* of letting go that deepened my ability to walk the Way of the Tao. I'd frequently say to myself, "Thank you (name) for giving me the gift of the practice of letting go." The practice itself propelled me into a new level of consciousness, where I began experiencing stillness.

Evening Reflection

Engaging in an evening reflection on my thoughts and actions of the day is a third way that I still my mind. I reflect on whether I've been in alignment or out of alignment with my love-power. I mentally note what I said or what action I took that was coming from love or fear. I note how I felt in the moment of saying or doing the action. The body always tells us if we are aligned with love or not. If I'm not aligned, I don't smile, and there's an odd sensation in my stomach as though I just ate something that I'm sensitive to. When I am aligned, joy fills my body, and I smile.

Notice your body's sensations when you're in your true power, as opposed to your distorted power, and record them. Once you recognize how you feel, you can make choices that put you back on track with your authentic power.

Another helpful way to get back on track is to ask yourself, "What is this really about?" As *A Course in Miracles* says, the problem is never what you think it is. Go deep in reflection of the fear and belief behind the event and people involved (hint: it's never about them). What past event does it remind you of? What power patterns are running up against each other (often between two or more people) just like in the past? What fear was created during this past event? What belief was created when you felt the fear? If this takes more than a few minutes during evening reflection time, simply schedule it in for the next day. But don't forget about it. You cannot arrive at stillness if you put off examining the cause of the chaos and imbalance.

Once you do the work to get clear about the primary belief underlying your upset, it's helpful to use a process to dissolve the belief; otherwise, it continues to show up. I recommend using the four questions of Byron Katie's "The Work." My son, Matthew McGregor, is an NLP master practitioner and has helped me with many of my beliefs as I became aware of what was getting in the way of my stillness. I'm also a big advocate of getting a coach who can guide you through frustration to self-awareness to shattering beliefs that no longer serve you. Michelle Falcone helps her clients see and break through unconscious "shadow" beliefs using the Shadow Process that the late Debbie Ford created to help people love and accept all parts of themselves. Whatever process you use, be sure to put your heart into it. Commitment yields results when a system has been proven to work. When we trust the process and follow through, we see changes that lead to more peace, joy, and the ability to be an influencer in the Way of the Tao.

The Impact of Time on Stillness

One of our primary relationships is our relationship with time. Our belief about time is fundamental to stillness, fulfillment, and joy. Do you feel squeezed for time? Do you feel that you never have enough time, that you are running out of time, that you could be using your time better? Do you feel like time has control over you?

Time is a construct of the mind that is designed to make us feel as though we are in control and, paradoxically, in constant fear of lack. In terms of power patterns, notice how the Controller wants to dominate, control others, control the environment, and even control God. The outcome typically appears as exhaustion, irritation, overwhelm, and ultimately, poor health. The truth is that all our dysfunctional patterns and beliefs around time are based in fear and, therefore, all stem from illusion.

If our many beliefs about time are an illusion, then what is the truth? I believe that human beings are just beginning to understand that time does not exist. There is significant scientific evidence that our universe is holographic, which means that we perceive that the world is three-dimensional, but the universe is based in two-dimensional coding, giving us a false perception of time and space. This theory, gaining strong support in the 1990s, shows growing evidence that our lifetimes may be simultaneous; we may be living multiple lives at the same "time" versus the common perception of having past lives. This suggests that time, as understood by humans, does not exist.

Knowing this, how can we live in a world that demands that we follow the rules of human time? I believe we can still agree to make our meetings, keep our deadlines, commit to following through by a certain timeframe, while still choosing not to be emotionally drawn in by the illusion of time. We don't need to feel a lack of time or the pressure of time. We can be mentally and emotionally free of the artificial construct by staying in our pure power and presence. Meditate, be aware of personal power patterns, and step into the commitment to step out of the matrix of illusion—all that is not unconditional love and all that is incongruent with the Way of the Tao. Imagine how your world would be if you no longer participated in this kind of matrix, and you could be fully present to people in your life, to your experiences, and to love. It would be heaven on earth!

The illusion of time and the fear that it generates robs us of the present moment. It takes away our ability to fully experience life and has us, in contrast, worried about death. In his book, *The Untethered Soul*, Michael Singer says, "You really don't need more time before death; what you need is more depth of experience during the time you're given." Come to an acceptance that your only role is to remain aware and let things move through you without holding on. Be like water, as Lao Tzu often remarked in the Tao. Flow with life and be present to it so that you feel as though you have really lived—no matter when you die.

Reflections

Journal about stillness in your life. When and where can you incorporate more stillness? When does your mind struggle to be still? Record how you feel after meditation or practicing gratitude daily for one week. Notice the difference in your state of peace, calm, and wellbeing. Then journal on your relationship with time and how it supports or prevents the level of stillness you seek. Notice how this awareness begins to shift you into a greater level of stillness. Celebrate even the smallest of personal improvements in this area. You are growing as you read this book, as you write in your journal and as you become even more of the change-maker you are called to be.

Seven

Stillness Strategies

Take on difficulties while they are still easy.
Do great things while they are still small.
Step by step the world's burden is lifted.
Piece by piece the world's treasure is amassed.

—Tao Te Ching, Verse 63

Establish Agreements and Boundaries

Setting clear agreements and boundaries in life contributes to stillness. Whether you are a parent, business owner, employee, or retired, your influence is in direct proportion to the agreements and boundaries you communicate. Knowing what a "No" is and what a "Yes" is allows you to be clear on your boundaries and what you will and won't do. It also means you have more time to dedicate to things that really matter.

If you are finding yourself in the same old dramas with your kids, or you're irritated by frequent interruptions at work or by people who don't follow through, it's likely that you haven't set up clear agreements about boundaries. Without agreements, one transgression occurs, and another, and shortly, there is a wildfire. It's in the smallest of agreements that the key to peace and calm reside.

Saying "No" can be incredibly freeing and lead to an environment of stillness. It can be as simple as choosing not to take on another project, join another association, or volunteer for a cause. It can be as difficult as setting boundaries in intimate relationships, creating boundaries with your children, or telling someone what you are no longer willing to do or accept. Whatever it is, saying "No" can free you from power dynamics, create spaciousness in your personal life, and return harmony to your life because you are honoring what's most important.

If you don't have agreements and boundaries, you act as if most requests, information, and events are worth giving your full time and attention to. But, as business trainer and speaker John Maxwell says, "You cannot overestimate the unimportance of practically everything." When it comes to stepping into being an influencer, the unimportant must be identified so that when it comes up in daily life, you have systems to deal with it. Each time you say "No," you strengthen what you do believe in and what you are willing to stand for. When you say "No" in this way, it is "for the good of all," and has far-reaching influence. Think of Rosa Parks saying, "No, I will not sit at the back of the bus." Her boundary, briefly and fully expressed, led to the expression of millions of people breaking free of the weight of racism and inequality.

Like Rosa Parks and the many people actively involved in the Black Lives Matter Movement, saying "No" may also involve taking a stand for what you will no longer accept in life or in society. Such as your own belief systems. Or your power patterns and those of others. Stories that have defined your life or negatively impacted the lives of others. "No more" is a powerful statement indicating that you're ready to make changes that will alter you and influence others. When you make a change from the commitment of saying "Never again," you give others hope that they can do the same.

The space that "No" creates allows you to have more focus, more discipline, and more follow-through. When I became vegan, along with the commitment to no longer eat unhealthy, "dead" food, I affirmed that I would lead a life of true health, vitality, and a harm-free lifestyle. My decision to say "No" to animal products and animal cruelty and say "Yes" to veggies and sustainability for the earth created space because I no longer thought about all the issues related to health and sustainability that crossed my mind as I danced around the idea of being vegan. I was also surprised by how many people said my decision inspired them to begin the same journey. Every choice and commitment is accounted for in this energetic universe. Mass change can begin with just a few people saying, "No more."

Follow Through

When I first entered the world of business two decades ago and became an entrepreneur offering personal development workshops, I quickly noticed what was blocking me from my goals. I'd repeatedly have "Big Ideas" (the Visionary), and I even began implementing those ideas, but I never followed through to complete them. Since I never followed through, I never had to say that I failed or that I made a mistake. My fear of being judged for trying to create something was so strong that I was perpetually telling people what I was up to, yet I was no further ahead in my dream from year to year. Lack of follow-through created frustration and chaos in my life and made me feel that I had little to no influence or impact in the world.

Teresa de Grosbois, founder of the Evolutionary Business Council and author of the bestselling book *Mass Influence*, shared with me that two of the biggest distinctions of the influential are that they are in action and are willing to make mistakes. She notes that carving out ten minutes a day consistently can add up to living your dreams and becoming the person that you want to be. However, most people don't do it because they are afraid to be wrong or to make mistakes. Teresa says, "Great influencers are not afraid to fail, not afraid for things to get messy. We are making it up as we go along. No plan survives first contact. Leaders are constantly adjusting and apologizing, and if you are not willing to spend five and ten minutes more per day…dreams will remain dreams, and influence will elude you."

People who are afraid to make mistakes eventually take on the Blamer energy, either in a passive-aggressive way or overtly, somehow conveying that it is other peoples' fault that they are not following through. By taking no responsibility, they get to be right and in control. This was my reality in the early years of my business. The Controller power pattern consumed me. It was the most difficult and most unhappy time of my life.

In working with thousands of entrepreneurs over the past decade, I've noticed the tendency to exhibit Shiny Object Syndrome also creates unsettled feelings and disharmony. This syndrome, driven by a fear of making mistakes and not being enough, leads highly creative people to avoid following through. They get caught up in the whirlwind of new ideas and new opportunities that justify their lack of follow-through. The syndrome originates from the distinct feeling of being stuck in life. When we feel this way, it is nearly impossible to quickly return to a sense of stillness. There is nothing more detrimental to self-esteem and confidence than not following through and not committing to that which is important to you.

In several conversations I had with Dr. John Demartini, he described how many people consider self-love to be quite complicated when it can be quite simple. That is, when you are doing what you love, when you have a commitment to follow through, and when you do what it takes to live according to what is most important to you, then you will feel self-love—and you will return to inner stillness. Midlife transitions and what some term "midlife crises" are simply opportunities to look at the alignment between what is most important to you and whether you are acting in ways that sustain that alignment.

People treat commitment and follow-through as old fashioned ideals and prefer to joke about Shiny Object Syndrome. Yet making a shift to following through can be the difference between feeling unsettled, irritated, and in a perpetual "something's missing" mindset and being fulfilled, peaceful, and in joy.

Great leaders follow through. The reason people follow them and continue to follow them long after their first contact is that they have what Music World owner and creator of Destiny's Child, Mathew Knowles, calls a high "Talk-To-Do ratio"—if they say they are going to do it, they do it. In my interview with him, he said, "Nothing hurts morale and spirit more than someone you look up to telling you they are going to do something, and then they don't do it. It's the responsibility of the influencer to follow up."

Mathew walks his talk. Later, during a retreat that I hosted in Italy with Michelle Falcone, I was surprised at how very generous Mathew was with his time and his willingness to share his connections to support my clients. I was even more delighted by the way in which he kept his word. He offered to make a call to connect two of our retreat members with a music producer, and he followed through with that offer on the spot. He also offered to be in personal contact with a budding speaker in our group and stayed true to his word with that person as well. I have never forgotten that gesture and the lesson of "Do what you say you are going to do…and quickly." Mathew's actions influenced me to the point that I began the practice of immediate follow-through whenever possible, and when not possible, within forty-eight hours. It builds trust and builds relationships that last.

Create Environmental Stillness

The more I practiced stillness by addressing my power patterns and my ego's needs that drive these patterns, the more I was aware that my physical environment exuded the opposite of stillness. It exhibited the old signs of a frenzied and chaotic existence. I had a sense that if I could just shift my physical environment, my inner world would also shift. At that point, I was rereading Malcolm Gladwell's *The Tipping Point*, in which the author shares studies to support his observations that our external environment causes changes in our internal environment. In one of these studies, Gladwell writes about William Bratton, who was appointed commissioner of the New York City Police Department after Rudolph Giuliani was elected mayor of New York City in 1994. Gladwell demonstrates how Bratton understood the power of a clean and non-violated environment.

Bratton helped to drastically cut down incidents of subway graffiti by not allowing even one car to go back out on the tracks after it had been defaced. He did the same with broken windows. By fixing windows again and again over a period of years, he sent the signal that the environment was to be respected. The incidents of vandalism drastically reduced.

This is not unlike Disney parks. Why are they so very clean? There is not a minute that goes by that someone is not quickly picking up garbage in every area of the Disney parks. When an environment is clean, we tend to respect it more and not be tempted to let a fly-away napkin just land somewhere. We care more. The opposite is also true. Take a clean desk, for example. It is much more likely that you will put a piece of paper in its proper place when your desk is clean and organized than when you have a stack of towering papers. We toss the paper onto the stack without a second thought.

Each time we add to the "stack"—whether it is physical or mental—we add more to our disorganized and chaotic mind. We are accepting the way it's always been. We begin to voice that things are "good enough." We may feel the temptation to return to old habits in regard to both training the mind and creating an environment of stillness. But if we take small steps toward establishing stillness on the outside of us, we can experience more internal peace, wellness, and harmony within.

Environmental stillness is also important to productivity and reaching goals because it enables us to exist in an environment that supports and honors creativity. Creativity is one of the most fundamental values of an influencer. By establishing stillness in life, we prepare to be in alignment with the highest creative vibration of the universe: love-power. All spiritual and religious traditions honor creation as the lifeblood of our existence, yet our environments need to reflect it.

To be in a creative space by creating stillness, observe each room that you use every day and notice what causes unsettling thoughts. Does your office lack a system for filing bills or random pieces of information? Do your bedroom clothes and accessories not have a "home"? Is your bathroom vanity a stage for fifty different "essentials," of which only five are used regularly? Are books piled high on your living room coffee table? Is your kitchen pantry filled with jars and cans that make it hard for you to find things with ease? These things do not promote stillness.

You might say, "I can train my mind to be peaceful in this mess." True, you can train your mind to do anything. But the question is: why make training your mind more challenging than it already is?

Take a sheet of paper and a pen now and take inventory. Section off the paper into categories that represent rooms in your home. One by one, go through each room and note anything you have looked at and thought about, even if for a second or two. For example, I walk into my kitchen and see a seed sprouting jar I bought three weeks ago, sitting on a shelf above the sink, still waiting to be used. Write down what you commit to doing about it and a date by which it will be done. Example: "Put the seeds in the jar and water this evening." Ideally, complete the first room in the first week, and then move to another room. The entire home can be completed within a few weeks, but the actions need to be marked in a calendar. This clearing process will prevent your mind from thinking the same thought over and over every day, with the added frustration of knowing that nothing will be done about it. That knowingness leads to disharmony, further frustration, and finally, stillness dissolves completely.

If you live with others, do this process together and you will learn much more about each other as you make decisions on what stays and what goes. Note if you or the other feels a sense of fear or control during this process. The simple awareness of this is often enough to support a healthy decision based in honoring stillness, or an unhealthy decision based in the need for control or safety.

Another way to minimize environmental chaos is to have a place for everything. When coming home from shopping, do you have a dedicated place for everything you buy? In other words, do many things end up in a "junk" drawer or closet, sending the signal that none of what you value is truly valued? What about gifts? Do you know where to put gifts so that they are honored and cherished, or do you treat them as dust collectors? If you don't like a gift, don't hold onto it. Everything in your home should be personally meaningful or useful.

Being clear about where things go can help create stillness because your home then feels sacred, solid, and reliable, rather than a dumping ground for whatever comes its way. Take inventory of each dedicated place in your home. Is it clearly a place for certain items? Or is it a chaotic mess? The more "junk drawer" storage, the less environmental stillness in your home.

I also create stillness in my environment by regularly giving things away that I no longer find beautiful or useful. If I haven't used something for six months, and it's not connected to my highest values of freedom, family, spirituality, or creation, I am quick to purge. I also don't add to my environment through excessive shopping. Most of the time, I stay away from shopping malls and tourist traps. The more we accumulate, the more blocked energy those things hold in our homes, and the less spaciousness is provided for our energetic field to create.

A clean and peaceful home encourages a clean and peaceful mind. Conversely, a still mind contributes to keeping the home and office free of physical clutter. In *The Life-Changing Magic of Tidying Up*, Marie Kondo says, "When we really delve into the reasons for why we can't let something go, there are only two: an attachment to the past or a fear for the future." When we train our minds to be still, we are training our minds to let go of the past, to forgive past incidents, and to release the control we desire over our future and the future of others.

Systems are also vital to organizational stillness. No matter what storm arises, well-designed systems with clear steps, structures, and agreements ensure unexpected chaos will not take you out. A simple example of having no system may look like this: "I can't find the keys. Where are the keys?" This is a question that confounded me for over four decades, but no more! I now have one dedicated place where I can quickly access my keys.

Forbes magazine reports that the typical executive wastes 150 hours annually searching for lost information. That is almost an entire month, every year! *Newsweek* reported that the average American wastes fifty-five minutes a day looking for things they own but can't find. Given these statistics, imagine how creating a system for finding things easily would greatly enhance your experience of stillness, rather than irritation, anxiety, and frustration.

An organizational consultant told me that the mind has preferences it is attached to, so using this to your advantage in finding things can be helpful. For example, when I began putting my keys in a beautiful crystal bowl, I remembered to do it consistently because my mind was drawn to the beauty of the bowl and I took extra care when placing the keys into it. Habits that work with our minds instead of against them are useful and can contribute to overall feelings of stillness and well-being.

Design Time Spaciousness

People often ask me how I can get so much done in such a small amount of time. I believe a major factor is that I've designed my life around a spaciousness of time and physical environment. I've created a training and speaking business that does not demand my time every day. During hours when most people are working on their business, or busy at the office, I take the time to write books and create new programs. Or I go on vacation and do research for my next big project. This space allows me the stillness required to create something that serves the world long after I'm gone.

If you don't have a great deal of flexibility in your career, consider how you might structure your time to create more stillness in your home space. Record how you are currently using your time from minute to minute for an entire week: this practice illuminates where changes can be made to support spaciousness. For more information on how to create more flexibility in your work or business, visit my site, www.SpeakerSuccessFormula.com.

Because of my own experience with the benefits of solitude, I have a strong belief that influence exists in people who practice solitude. I have always created my most powerful talks, segments of books, and new ideas when setting aside alone time. Not easy, yet essential. Pablo Picasso reflected, "Without great solitude, no serious work is possible." Carve out time not only to vacation but to be utterly and completely alone. This is far from a vacation for many people. The bliss of complete solitude lasts about three days, and then they crave distraction. Truly, three days is not stillness; it is entering silence. Yet there is a difference between silence and stillness. When becoming still, you transition from the quiet of not being busy or distracted to the spiritual experience of knowing who you really are. In this knowing, you create your masterpiece. In this knowing, you create and leave a legacy.

If you are wondering how on earth you are going to "find the time" for solitude, consider Bill Gates, one of the busiest, most in-demand people on the face of the earth, who carves out one week every year to simply think. In my opinion, Bill is doing more than just thinking; he is activating solitude to discover what really matters. Jeff Weiner, CEO of LinkedIn, schedules up to two hours of solitude daily. In this space, he thinks about what really matters for his company and comes back to emotional balance.

Over a decade ago, I interviewed one of Vancouver, Canada's top entrepreneurs, Brian Scudamore, of 1-800-GOT-JUNK fame, and more recently, Shack Shine. He told me of a time when he was struggling to make his business successful. He decided to spend one week at his parents' cabin alone, out on the pier, reconstructing his entire vision for his junk removal business. This solitude gave him what he needed to create the global success of Got Junk. In my interviews with other entrepreneurs, they also said they made better decisions and were more creative when they entered a period of stillness. Stillness allows the brain to take a back seat to what really wants to come through. It allows for intuition, creativity, and flow, all of which are Sacred experiences of influencers who walk the path of the Tao. Carving out regular chunks of time is important, yet longer periods of a week to a month of solitude are ideal.

Honor Simplicity

Reduce what you have. Decrease what you want.

—Tao Te Ching, Verse 19

To support a state of stillness, one of the habits I've developed in all areas of life is simplicity. If my business has too many product offerings, I streamline to offer only one or two. When my kids were younger and wanted to try out a new sport or program, I made sure (for my sons and for me) that only one thing was explored at a time. I remember being one of the few parents who did not believe in filling every minute of my children's time with activities. Give kids room to just be! The levels of stress and depression in young kids are at an all-time high; I don't recall any of my friends growing up feeling that way. I do remember taking long walks along the railway tracks, talking about boys, singing songs in the big prairie fields, and playing with other kids while our moms dropped in to a neighbor's house for coffee. Life was much simpler.

"But all of that has changed. We are not in that world any longer," you might say. And while this is partly accurate, most of us have chosen to make our lives anything but simple. We take a job that we know will be a massive time commitment and potential energy drain. We fall in love with the person who is full of drama and then choose to stay in the relationship. We follow in the footsteps of other families and buy our kids more and more electronics and gadgets that sit around collecting dust after a few months. We look around our home and wonder how it got to be so chaotic. So much busy-ness, so many possessions, so many roller-coaster rides of emotion and tension. We feel tired and exhausted just thinking about it all.

And yet the need for more is so strong because our ego has convinced us that we must do more, buy more, and achieve more to be deemed worthy and to have a semblance of control over our lives. I was once that way; I thought that if I just had the top job, married a good husband, and had a good home with well-behaved children, I could relax knowing that I was enough. When my marriage fell apart, and I lost the business that I co-created with two friends, I realized that nothing is permanent. I realized that I could try my best, but there was still no guarantee that the outcome would go as planned.

So, I began to design a new, simple life for myself. A life I would love with no room for "busy, overwhelmed, and dramatic." I would create simplicity in every aspect of my world. This simplicity would elevate my creative time, my joy, and my connection with others since it created space to be in the present moment.

I got rid of most of my clothes, binders, and books that weren't being used. I got rid of wall art, kitchen gadgets, and garage boxes that I was holding "just in case." With each purge, I felt more free. And freedom is my top value, so I knew that the commitment to live a simple life was nurturing who I was at my core.

More recently, I've changed the way I interact with my cell phone to bring more simplicity into my life. Studies show that people interact with their cell phones on average 150 times per day, and the top percentile almost six hundred times per day. That means we are living life largely through the filter of a tiny screen that's sending us information that we deem important. When we interact with our phones to this degree, our minds become filled with not only all the things we need to do that day, but all the things we hope to do, all the people we must get back to, and the latest viral laughing baby videos. From Facebook, Instagram, LinkedIn, and Snapchat to our favorite apps, texts, phone calls, and emails—we are held hostage by our phones. I once posted on Facebook that my favorite wisdom is, "Be still and know that I am God," not "Be still and know that I am your cell phone." We lose hope of simplicity when we become addicted to our mobile devices; stillness is long gone.

Many people develop addictive tendencies, with more and more joining the mass rising of social media addiction. In the quest to be seen, appreciated, and loved, many spend hours a day on social feeding power patterns like these:

- Victim—shares anything and everything that happens that could be seen as "poor me" or "poor us"

- Martyr—looks at all the good they're doing in the world

- Savior—scours posts to see who is looking for help or posts a Victim story we can engage in

- Chosen One—is certain that what they've done or written no one has ever done before

- Judge—looks for any instance to disagree with a post

- Blamer—posts publicly and in groups about those at fault who shall not be named, providing just enough information so everyone knows who it is

- Withdrawer—makes sure everyone knows that they'll remove friends who don't interact with or see their posts. Occasionally announces that they are taking a break from social media because they can't deal with the "morons" in cyberland.

- Controller—on the lookout for anyone who violates their rules of social media and has all the filters in place to make sure they're in control. They're also suspicious and fearful that their private information might be abused.

Can you see how each power pattern has its unique way of using social media and mobile devices to justify behavior? Take some time to create new agreements for yourself about interacting with mobile devices and social media that support your stillness and allow you to live a simple life.

I am fully committed to following through with choices that nurture simplicity. My commitment has allowed me to grow a successful business, live the lifestyle I choose for myself, and nurture my connection to my children—all with joy and gratitude. If a new opportunity presents itself and is not simple in concept, I'm not interested. Freedom of time and space that gives me the ability to create the life I want is more important than any complicated journey, no matter what the outcome at the end of the day.

In my work as a trainer and speaker, I find that people who choose complexity over simplicity are not in touch with their hearts and intuition. They are listening only to the reasoning part of their minds, which typically complicates decisions and often encourages them to follow what others are doing. They end up not knowing their purpose and feel lost and directionless. They may have a great passion for their job or business for a while, but it doesn't last because they have not created the space and simplicity to see who they really are at their core.

You are now ready to dive into the third pillar of influence: Purpose. In Part III: Purpose, we explore the types of purpose and how they can influence your life and the lives of those you touch. We'll look at the barriers to understanding our purpose and how to break through to clarity. We'll also explore steps that influencers can take to help others recognize their own purpose to produce positive change.

Reflections

Take time to journal about how much stillness you experience in your life. Have you designed a life that reduces stillness? Have you made decisions that give you sufficient time to create the next phase of your life and be the influencer you have come here to be? List all the fears that may be getting in the way of honoring your sacred time and your need for stillness.

List all the environmental factors that have worked against stillness in your life. Make a commitment to focus on eliminating or reducing these factors. At the same time, let yourself feel the fear deeply and then choose to move on, knowing that the fear is trying to keep you safe from change. Create a mantra that grounds your commitment to stillness. "Be still and know that I am God," or "This too shall pass," are examples of supportive mantras. Choose what works for you and repeat in times when you are experiencing chaos in your mind. In your journal, record your "wins" and your insights that came about as a result of making commitments to your stillness and saying your mantra regularly.

Pillar III

Purpose

Eight

Understanding Purpose

One who lives in accordance with nature does not go against the way of things. He moves in harmony with the present moment, always knowing the truth of just what to do.

—Tao Te Ching, Verse 8

When most people think of "purpose," they think of their job or career. While that may be a part of one's purpose, it's only one aspect of it. For years, I taught people to discover their career purpose, and as the curriculum for the courses developed, I realized how expansive purpose actually is. Purpose is both a human, earthly concept and a Divine reality. With that in mind, I began to see three distinct categories of purpose, or what I call first, second, and third-level purpose. First-level purpose has to do with survival, the overriding goal being to provide safety from possible external threats. Second-level purpose has to do with aligning your inner whispers and soul guidance—those pertaining to a vision, mission, or calling—with the external environment. Second-level purpose is the primary focus of this chapter. Third-level purpose is expressed as a state of pure love-power—when one exists as love itself and chooses actions that are based on unconditional love. We will explore third-level purpose in Chapter 10.

First-Level Purpose

First-level purpose is what many of our parents or grandparents lived through. Their goal was to have a reasonably stable and safe life with food on the table, children taken care of, bills paid, and, if they were fortunate enough, money left over to help those in need. While first-level purpose may not seem as prevalent in the Western world today, the same fears that drove our ancestors continue to drive us today. For example, many of us still have a fear of never having enough. When a parent has a profound fear about surviving on the physical dimension, their children will absorb it and may subconsciously hold the same worries and fears as their parents and grandparents—whether or not conditions have changed for the better.

The science of epigenetics, which studies how genes can be altered or turned on or off by our internal and external environment, has been central to our understanding of generational patterns of behavior. It can take up to seven generations before a belief system that's fear-based is woven out of the fabric of reality within a family. In other words, the external environment for the next generation may change significantly, but the beliefs that cause a similar pattern of behavior do not. Children of these families often grow into adults who are controlled by thoughts focused on financial lack. Then they usually do one of two things: overcompensate for their fear by doing anything for money—i.e., become a Controller to make sure they win in the game of finances—or complain about being tired, broke, and never able to get ahead due to the "powers that be." The latter group becomes Victims and often Blamers. (After all, it's someone else's fault that they are unhappy with their financial state!) Over time, both groups discover that the majority of their energy is consumed by emotions and thoughts connected to financial survival and regret that they've spent much of their lives unhappy because of it.

If these individuals continue to live out their lives with a primary purpose of survival, they will never feel fulfillment, joy, and vitality. Their only hope is to begin examining their own power patterns, as described earlier in this book. They need to look at why they've developed these patterns and recognize that their strong survival fears are based on a perception that may have been true in the past—but not now. They need to begin practicing healthy daily habits, such as meditation and letting go of disempowering thoughts. When these people begin distancing themselves from the thoughts that once controlled them, they will be ready to experience second-level purpose.

If you are a leader involved in developing a team and hiring and firing people, you already know the importance of choosing people who operate higher than first-level purpose. If you don't, you'll be challenged by lack of commitment, low retention rates, high absenteeism, and a culture of complaining and blaming. You'll have two choices: choose people who have a second-level purpose or higher or make a commitment to develop a training program that helps your first-level purpose employees get beyond it and choose to see that life has meaning beyond survival.

Second-Level Purpose

Those with a second-level purpose have not escaped the ego's demands and fears, but they do have a yearning to do something with their lives that has personal meaning and serves others. Still, society has muddied the waters by being obsessed with the notion that people must be "special" when it comes to their purpose. But it's just not so. If we think we have some special purpose while others don't, we can fall into the Chosen One power pattern. "I will save the world! Just watch me!" says a Chosen One. It becomes all about "me"—and to a much lesser extent about "us."

Our culture has also confused the notion of purpose by thinking that it must be accompanied by a certain degree of clarity. Lack of clarity is seen as an embarrassing flaw, and people often judge it harshly. The only way to recognize purpose, many believe, is by the dazzling clarity an individual has about their purpose, along with the ability to speak about it in depth. But it doesn't necessarily work that way. Some people are simply in a transition to find their purpose, and an openness to that transitional period supports their efforts. Imagine if we stopped viewing others as "lost" on their journey and saw them as being on the greatest journey of their lives, filled with opportunity and experiences.

> *Things that are forced grow for a*
> *while but then wither away.*
>
> **—Tao Te Ching, Verse 55**

Due to society's attitudes, it can be painful if we don't have clarity about our purpose. But if you let the fear of not being enough control you, you weaken your ability to make change in your life and to influence others to make a better world. Additionally, you make fear-based decisions, resulting in distorted power, instead of making decisions based on your love-power. Ultimately, by doing so, you trade in your soul's calling and purpose for comfort, security, or the respect of the tribe—and inevitably experience emptiness and apathy as a result.

The Five Organic Stages of Clarity

If you're in that in-between phase, transitioning to a higher frequency of living, but you don't know your purpose yet, it can be uncomfortable. It's a time when people are often more likely to settle for an existence that doesn't fully align with who they are. They do so only because they don't understand the cycle of clarity. They hold on to familiar ways of being, which can lead to living a life they never wanted. Their lives become bearable or "good enough" until the stirrings of the soul can no longer be denied without consequence.

But our souls are naturally beckoning us to grow into our purpose—and we are given the clarity we need to do so. Clarity evolves organically, helping us to understand ourselves and the ways we will serve the world. It helps us to feed our soul instead of our fearful mind, which only keeps our old patterns in place.

The clarity that organically evolves within us is comprised of five stages. Each stage influences how well we transition from one stage to the next. The whole cycle of clarity may not be easy to complete, but it is critical if we are to shift from a fear-governed life to a soul-governed life.

STAGE ONE: RELEASE AND GRIEVE

We first must release what was. Even if we don't like our past circumstances, the people and events that occurred were a significant part of our lives. We may feel angry or disappointed, and we may want to push it all away, but what is not felt and released will continue to block our clarity, and we will get stuck, missing the opportunity to transition into something that excites us.

As a spiritual seeker, you might be hesitant to go back to the past because the present moment is with all that is God. However, unless you're enlightened—which is extremely rare—your mind returns to the past frequently. The frustration of staying "stuck in the muck" remains because you haven't cleared anything; you've only pushed it aside. Fortunately, it's not too difficult to deal with. To do so, allow all the feelings of your past to present themselves. It may take a few days to become familiar with all the different sensations that want to be released. Allow the process to unfold. It can be challenging to allow your body to feel and release without your mind getting hooked into the emotion, feeding the ego's needs, and magnifying your power patterns.

Since my spiritual awakening involving Mother Mary, I know that pain can be released through the portal of the heart. In fact, when you focus on your heart, a desire to release the pain of the past often arises. Even better, your heart knows how to do that without your mind interrupting. Here's how: Put your attention on your heart and notice that it feels warm or even hot. That is a sign you are releasing stored emotional pain. It is a physical process that connects your soul's will—the will to surrender fear and return to the reality of love—with your heart's will to release your body of painful energy that is not based in love. At this point in the cycle of clarity, the mind has no role. It's helpful to remind yourself of that, ensuring your heart completes its function to release grief and open you to the next phase of clarity.

STAGE TWO: BECOME COMFORTABLE WITH THE UNKNOWN

The second stage of evolving clarity is about becoming comfortable with the unknown. The universe begins sending you the message that in order to grow and impact many lives, you need to live in accordance with Universal Laws. As outlined in Chapter One, one of those Universal Laws is the Law of Change. As we release what once was, and move toward what will be, there is a space—it is the unknown, the great void. For most people, it is the most challenging space to be in. Admitting that you don't know where you're headed can rear up the ego's defense mechanisms and fuel resistance to the Law of Change.

Because of the fearful feelings that arise from a mind trying to avoid change, many people choose to settle. The "pressure" they feel from their own minds, combined with conditioning from parents, institutions, and colleagues to make a "sensible" choice, often creates a tipping point that leads to making a hasty decision that is not aligned with the soul. I've seen many people in job and relationship transitions quickly choose another partner or another job that virtually mimics what they had previously—only with slight renovations giving the illusion of an upgrade. This often leads to that old familiar feeling of being stuck and frustrated once again.

To more easily move through the stage of The Unknown, let yourself become very quiet. Sit in a meditative state and see the universe as black space—no sound, no lights, no images, no sensations. Be a witness to the enormous space unfolding in your awareness. Breathe this space into your body and let the unknown fill you. As your mind attempts to interject with its ploys to keep you safe, simply relax even further and let the thoughts pass by. Stay with the present moment of the unknown. Focus only on this moment: now.

The more we practice being with the unknown, the more we can feel one with it and the entire universe. This unity consciousness brings a level of peace that few people have ever experienced. When we have dealt with our power patterns and have disengaged from our ego's needs, what is left is the peace of our love-power.

Operating from love-power, we are comfortable with the unknown because it is part of a loving universe that supports us in ways the mind will never know.

STAGE THREE: ENTER THE SPACE OF POSSIBILITY

A world of possibility begins to take place as we surrender to the unknown. Literally, we are more creative as we move from a chaotic, incoherent brain wave pattern (caused by the untrained monkey mind) to one that is steady and coherent. Dr. Joe Dispenza has devoted his life to studying the brain and understanding the science behind it to produce better results for people in all areas of life. He notes that when the brain's energy is divided between many objects, people, problems, and issues, there is no energy left to create something new. To create something new, it is vital to train the brain to not only let go of the old ways of being but to step into creating a new reality.

This new reality can be stimulated in many ways. I have found the most effective way to begin creating my reality is to take time every day to envision what I value and love doing. If your clarity of purpose has not yet come into focus, you might wonder how you can see what you're not clear about. From helping hundreds of entrepreneurs to arrive at clarity, I know that once they've experienced the first two stages, they find it effortless to imagine the impact they'll have on others as they serve in a new way. They may not know the "how" yet, but they understand their potential to influence and leave a legacy.

One effective method to create a new reality is to visualize possibilities without forcing them to happen. In other words, when in a meditative state, set the intention to see, feel, or know the Big Picture of the next phase of your life. Allow your inner eye to see what arises in that space. Don't grab hold of the image in your mind, as you will attempt to give it some sort of meaning, and, as a result, stop the flow of impressions. Your visions may not be as orderly as the mind prefers, but that's okay. Watch the mind wanting to hook into an image, but don't allow it. You always have the power to stop it. As the images or sensations come to an end, write down in your journal (dedicated to this next phase of your life) the guidance you received.

STAGE FOUR: ASK AND RECEIVE

Once you begin accessing the impressions that are designed to help you with clarity every day, ask for help through prayer or connecting with your Divine guides or a spiritual master. Ask to be given clear signs of the best direction to take. Or ask for events that give you the experience of what you visualized in your meditations. If you are now clear on your second-level purpose, ask for assistance in accessing the right information, meeting the right people, and making the best choices to elevate your impact.

Those who have the Withdraw, Martyr, or Controller power patterns will notice how difficult it is to step forth and ask or claim any kind of support. When we are used to removing ourselves from people and life, doing everything for everyone else, or pushing and insisting things go our way, we won't be able to ask and receive. That's why many people going through a life transition cannot gain clarity. The mind literally won't allow clarity to enter because it rules them—they don't rule it. The power patterns block the movement forward into the unknown and into change.

When it comes to asking and receiving, be aware of the power patterns that arise and record which types of support you have difficulty receiving. Replace your tendency to block the goodness and support that appear in your life with the habit of gratitude. Gratitude is the best way for you to acknowledge assistance from anyone or anything; it is also the best way for you to feel full acceptance of this new and wonderful time that is coming into form. If you experience a fear that the goodness will be taken away, simply observe the thought and, as always, let it float by while remaining unattached to its energy. Immediately return to a state of gratitude and fill your body with feelings of being blessed in every way.

STAGE FIVE: MAKE MISTAKES

The final stage of clarity comes when we are willing to make mistakes.
Each time we transition to the next phase of life and align with our
purpose more deeply, we may have some fear about action toward our
purpose. In working with many fledgling business owners, I have seen
the direct impact of fear around making mistakes. One outcome of the
fear may be procrastination, but there is another outcome that's even
more detrimental: creating confusion where there is none.

Many entrepreneurs create confusion unnecessarily. Some, for no
apparent reason, suddenly decide to take another training that has
nothing to do with their current direction. Off they go to study
some new modality or apparent upgrade to what they already
know, convinced that it will be the answer to their lack of clarity.
They inevitably return to me, saying, "I'm confused. I don't know
what to do."

Others do step into their purpose, but at the first sign of things not
going well, they say, "You know, I wasn't meant to do this. Clearly,
I'm being shown a sign." The only sign they are being shown is their
lack of commitment to deal with their thoughts and feelings around
making mistakes. They constantly use their environment and the
Divine as excuses that this new transition was simply not meant to
be. No influential human being who fulfilled their purpose ever said,
"This road is tough. Since I can't make a mistake, I'm just not going to
bother following through."

To alleviate the fear of making mistakes, acknowledge the good
intention behind the fear, which is to hide the original wound of
illusion that you're not enough. Sit with any remaining grief around
incidents in which you felt inadequate or that you had done something
wrong. Let the pain of those moments burn through your heart
and, without attaching further thoughts to the feelings, allow the
pain to release through your heart. Now your awareness will help

you see more clearly how you run from greatness by saying that you are confused.

You are not confused. In fact, you were never confused. You were only pushing against the natural flow of life that supports change aligned with the call of your soul.

UGG founder Brian Smith shares similar wisdom with his audiences. "Your most disappointing disappointments will always become your greatest blessings," he says. Mistakes are meant to move you toward the blessings of life, not away from them. Move with the natural flow of life and avoid getting stuck in disappointment. The gift is right around the corner.

Children and Second-Level Purpose

While facilitating a retreat in Italy, I asked Mathew Knowles, our guest speaker, how he parented Beyoncé and Solange in such a way that they both became renowned artists in the world of music while still retaining their great passion for performing and creating music. This is what he had to say:

> Surround your children with a lot of career choices at a very young age. In a childlike way—if it's an instrument, see if they enjoy playing it. If they like singing, get a vocal coach. Surround them with influencers and let the child make that decision. I teach a lot of students who hate what they are doing because their parents are making them do it. I have a lot of students that want to be in the music industry, but their parents won't allow them to be artists, so they are getting a degree that is the closest they can get to it.

When children are exposed to many career choices at a young age, they're more likely to tune into their soul's calling. Unfortunately, sometimes teachers can create self-doubt in children. Mathew continued, "Because teachers are around our children more than we are, they really have a lot of influence. There were many times when teachers asked Beyoncé and Solange, 'Why are you wasting your time with music?' So, I got on the school board so that I could build a relationship with their teachers."

Mathew's extraordinary actions ensured that Beyoncé and Solange would have the greatest opportunity to express their souls' calling. As parents, we can do the same. Our leadership influences future generations to lead organically and to be in the flow with the way we humans are designed—to respond to a deeper calling to manifest what wants to emerge through us. By using the five stages in the cycle of clarity, you will find that both confusion and clarity are, in the end, merely constructs of the mind. In the end, there is only Truth.

Reflections

Journal about the stage of clarity you have with second-level purpose. Can you see where you got stuck wondering about your second-level purpose because you didn't know these stages were natural and to be experienced? How can you help someone struggling to reach their second-level purpose? Who do you know that might need help with one or more of the stages of clarity? Can you have a conversation with them? Begin to be an influencer by taking time to support others, even if you are going through the process yourself.

Nine

Leading with Purpose

Know this Primal Power that guides without forcing,
that serves without seeking, that brings forth and
sustains life, yet does not own or possess it.

—Tao Te Ching, Verse 10

Business leaders often have high expectations of the people that work for them yet are occasionally disappointed by those who haven't clarified their purpose or identified their soul's calling. Many people gain employment by stumbling upon a job that pays well and has good benefits. But if that is their motivation, they are unlikely to exhibit mastery in their work. If there's a misalignment between what they are doing in their careers and what they were meant to do with their lives, it will show.

I believe that leaders need to be on the lookout for people who are not "on their dime." They need to have honest conversations with those who are not in alignment with their work. They need to help others see that they're not operating at their best if, in fact, that's the case.

When I spoke with Mathew Knowles, I was struck by his willingness to see that the difficult decision to let someone go is a gift, not a negative situation. He told me about a time when he spoke with a young man, one of his employees, who wasn't passionate about his role. As a result, Mathew decided to fire him. At first, the employee was angry, but months later, he came back and thanked Mathew for having the wisdom and courage to let him go. The young man was far happier and more passionate in his new career direction and just needed someone else to initiate the change.

I've been surprised many times by how second-level purpose shows up. Often the most difficult times in my life have led to the most profound realizations and change in direction that fulfilled my purpose. When I was going through divorce, I felt guilt and shame, thinking that I could have done more or tried harder to keep the marriage together. A few years later, I had a mystical experience that showed me that, on a soul level, my former husband was not the victim, but the hero in my life. He had gifted me with an opportunity to no longer rely on him financially and to have the confidence to build my dream life using my own skills, talents, and determination. In the depths of despair, I discovered the resources and strength I needed within me to follow my soul's calling.

In my years as a professional intuitive, I found that at least 50 percent of the people who came to me for private consultations were not fulfilled or joyful. They were trying to make up for ignoring their soul's calling by entering yet another relationship, rescuing yet another friend from a drama, or creating a new project at home to avoid their pain. Distractions were their go-to resource to deny that there was something very wrong in their lives. When the pain could no longer be masked, they reached out to me.

One highly successful business woman wanted to know what she should do with her life. She knew her current projects were not fulfilling, yet she was stuck because she didn't want to give up on what she perceived to be an incomplete venture. Having been a professional athlete and having wildly succeeded in every business she touched, the idea of moving on to something else was deeply unnerving to her. It represented failure.

I told her that real failure only happens when she's out of touch with her dreams or when she's not following them. True failure is not having the courage to let go of all that is out of alignment with her soul's calling. The only way she could fail would be to not take the leap into what was calling her heart.

She said didn't know what was calling her. Yet, I rarely find this to be the case with highly driven businesspeople. For most of them, they've been aware of a theme—a thread of knowing—that presented itself many times but was quieted through a lack of stillness, or a chaotic mind, or both. I reminded her how passionate and alive she became when she spoke about the inspiring non-profit for which she served on the board. She said she would love to be involved more in implementing its vision, but she didn't know how. I invited her to propose a new position that would both pay her well and demonstrate that she had the skill set required to grow the project to a globally renowned organization. She accepted my challenge. In the process, she reminded herself that no matter the outcome, she was succeeding, not failing, because she was aligning herself with her innermost calling.

No surprise: magic unfolded! My client was awarded one of the top executive positions in the company, and today, she influences millions of lives, tackling some of the largest global challenges. When we leaders influence others to make the world a better place, our job on this planet has been worthwhile.

Activating Community Callings

Second-level purpose often evolves into extending one's individual calling into working in a community with a common intention. It includes the awareness of working together, collaborating, envisioning, and acting toward the greater good. It often requires a higher level of consciousness, because to participate in the call toward doing things for the greater good, we need to drop the fears that keep us stuck in the need for personal recognition and security.

Saviors who drop their need for recognition and acceptance often lead the way in making a difference. Controllers who relinquish the need to be right and to have things go their way serve the greater good. Chosen Ones who drop the need to be special can be a force for good in seeing everyone who supports the cause as equal. Second-level purpose gets expressed in people who create, join, and sustain movements, volunteer to be leaders on boards of nonprofit organizations, or get involved in initiatives that support the people and planet.

If there are enough people in these groups who contribute at the level of "we" and not "I," miracles and breakthroughs happen. But if the majority are still stuck in power patterns, then the initial powerful vision and intentions cannot materialize or help transform the paradigms and structures that no longer serve communities and humanity at large.

In their book, *Option B,* Sheryl Sandberg and Adam Grant share what can happen when non-profit organizations work together to achieve a purpose that creates the ripple effect needed to solve big world problems. In a poverty-stricken area in India, a program called Girls First addresses many of the real challenges faced by the girls of the region. Most of them are not able to complete twelve years of education, and 70 percent get pregnant before they are eighteen years old. These challenges are overcome, in part, because the girls learn to identify and practice their unique strength of character, such as creativity, kindness, humility, and gratitude. Sandberg and Grant write:

> Girls who attended just one hour a week over six months saw their emotional resilience climb. During one session, an eighth grader named Ritu learned that bravery was one of her strengths. Soon afterward, she intervened to stop a boy from harassing her friends, and when her

father tried to make her ninth-grade sister get married, Ritu spoke up
and convinced him to wait.

Steve Leventhal, who runs Girls First, says, "Our work is to turn on
a light… The girls often say that no one had ever told them they
had strengths."

These acts of human kindness are more than just an idea or a
compassionate individual reaching out. The influence that such
programs generate happens because the people who comprise this
organization have a greater purpose beyond their individual purpose,
and they are present to the girls as they face enormous obstacles.
When people embody the drive of their second-level purpose and have
minimized the power patterns within themselves that often destroy
the goodwill of an organization, they create an environment where
humanity's toughest problems can be addressed and potentially healed.

Creating a Second-Level Purpose Team

The concepts in this book are hopefully opening your mind and heart
to the ways in which you can lead as a self-governed, conscious being,
responding to the call of your soul to fulfill your second-level purpose.
Activating this purpose is a prerequisite to leading a purpose-driven
team. Yet many leaders find that their purpose wanes to some degree
at some point in their lives, so they have to continually be in touch
with their souls' guidance and intuition to keep a clear direction and
maintain a powerful energy. Transition for a leader can be scary, but
your team will respect you for taking time to reflect deeply on your
path and where it needs to be tweaked or turned over completely.
Being honest with yourself and letting your soul lead the way does
ultimately produce the best long-term results.

One way to make sure that you and your team are fully aligned with your second-level purpose is to take inventory of everyone's level of commitment and passion for their work—your own and that of your employees, contractors, and colleagues. Rate everyone on a scale of one to ten for commitment and for passion. Add up the scores, and if someone scores lower than what is necessary to move the organization positively forward, consider having a conversation with them about your observations. Use language that is non-confrontational and void of defensiveness.

One template to assist in this process is this:

> [Name], I noticed that [state a fact], I imagine that [state what you are assuming]. Is that accurate?" [Allow the person to respond.]

For example, it might sound like: "John, I noticed you have been looking at your phone to check the time several times during our last few meetings. I imagine that this project doesn't interest you. Is that accurate?"

Another example:

> Amanda, I noticed that you contributed your thoughts and ideas two or three times during our meetings in the past, but during the last three meetings, you have been silent. I imagine that you are upset or angry with someone or something. Is that accurate?" [Allow the person to respond.]

By practicing stating a fact, stating what you perceive to be true, and then requesting clarification, you leave the door open for others to share from the heart and get to the heart of the matter.

We live in a society where many people are hurting because of one of two scenarios: they have found themselves in a job that is not the right fit for them, or they have created a business that doesn't align with their values and desired lifestyle. Most people feel trapped and silenced when this happens. They don't feel they can share their lack of enthusiasm with their boss or colleagues for fear of losing what they already have. They soldier on with repressed sadness and bottled anger. And we wonder why people are not productive! A happy workplace is a productive workplace. One of the greatest sources of happiness is knowing we are on track with our life's purpose—knowing we are acting on the whispers of our soul's calling.

The consequences of staying stuck in careers that are not fulfilling can be seen all around us. Canada has one of the highest rates of cancer in the world, yet it has one of the best healthcare systems. The US suffers from more heart disease than any other country, yet it has some of the best medical care in the world. I'm not suggesting that all cancer and heart disease are a result of refusing to follow the soul's calling, but I am inviting you to consider that disease is likely to happen when we are "heartbroken" with perceived helplessness. When there is even one courageous step toward letting go of what's no longer working and moving toward what you want, there can be tremendous gains in physical, mental, and emotional wellbeing.

As a leader, be willing to let go of "talent" if the person clearly has a purpose that is not being fulfilled within the organization. Sometimes, a new position in the same company may be more suitable to this talented individual; watch them light up in energy and passion as they explore something closer to their calling.

When I was giving life purpose workshops, people often approached me with low energy and complained about being tired at work. I remember having the same feeling as a teacher, although I didn't know at the time that my extreme fatigue was due to my work being a mismatch with my soul's calling. While I consider myself a teacher to this day, the environment and expectations in traditional schools were too restrictive for my entrepreneurial nature, which requires great freedom to create and express my work in my own way.

One clear sign that someone is aligned with a particular type of work and work environment is the energy they have when they talk about it. Their eyes light up, their body straightens up, they become more animated, and they seem to laugh and smile much more. As an influencer, be sure to share such behaviours when you witness them, not only within your team, but also at home with kids, friends, or family. Your willingness to influence others by sharing what you observe can be life-changing for them. In fact, many of the world's greatest leaders found themselves pivoting in a big way because someone was generous enough to notice and express the potential they saw in them that they didn't see in themselves.

As a leader, take time to tune into the purpose of others and ask questions about their passions. That feeling—the spirit of purpose—arises in the body and ignites passion. Invite people to see the possibility of getting to a new level of excellence. While it may seem out-of-place in many workplaces to ask people to get in touch with what they feel, feeling is the key to excellence. And when feeling one's emotions is combined with training the mind, influence naturally emerges. When we're clear about our purpose, the passion for creating (both individually and collaboratively) is infinite. The road to excellence may be challenging, yet it arises swiftly when a leader helps the team align with their purpose. Without purpose and the feeling generated by purpose, a masterpiece often goes unpainted.

A note about people who are not clear and committed to their purpose in life: many people unknowingly create chaos in their personal and professional lives to avoid stepping into their greater purpose. When people are not on track with their purpose, behaviors like anger, gossip, lying, adultery, addiction, indecisiveness, chronic lateness, interrupting conversations, and not listening to others can show up. You will undoubtedly recognize some of these behaviors in your colleagues or team, but it is just as important to reflect on which of these behaviors you find in yourself. Often, we are passionate and clear on where we are headed and why, but we use dysfunctional behaviors to slow us down, preferring to believe we are not enough or that we're unworthy. It takes deep humility for a leader to recognize patterns of belief and behaviors that stop their own light from shining and influencing others. Yet we all must be willing to go there if we are to be influencers of a higher order.

Creating a Purpose-Driven Team

When a team works together toward a mutually-inspiring purpose, it can be unstoppable. For this to happen, the team leader needs to nurture eight principles that are in keeping with the Taoist philosophies of love, balance, compassion, understanding, and openness. These are:

- Love them
- See them
- Ask questions
- Share what you see
- Invite conversations
- Mentor to excellence
- Support the "Learn What You Know" Principle
- Demonstrate leadership

LOVE THEM

Loving your team can sometimes seem simple, and other times seem impossible. It is why so much of this book talks about learning to train the mind. When it comes to working with others, whether employees, bosses, or colleagues, it is vital to make a commitment to truly love them. In a work environment, this can mean taking the first step

to understanding and accepting them as they are. Taking the time
to understand the circumstances, behaviors, and thought patterns
of others makes it easier to love them. It doesn't mean putting up
with abuse, procrastination, or a host of other unwelcome activity. It
means being able to observe with compassionate curiosity. Who is this
individual, really?

SEE THEM

In previous pages, I described the importance of presence in
influencing others. Here's where the rubber meets the road. When
present with others, we naturally see others for who they are. Without
filters, there are no judgments to cloud or distort perception. In
spiritual terms, the soul is seen; we begin to see the beauty inherent
in them. When we master being present, we see others regardless of
their behavior, regardless if they are being stubborn, irritating, or off-
putting. We see the being, not the behavior.

I'm not suggesting you invest your time and energy in working with
people who are consistently behaving in ways that disrupt the flow of
business. I'm inviting you to see beyond the ego's fears and judgments
and see the light in everyone you meet. That is when *doing* influence
turns to *being* an influencer.

ASK QUESTIONS

When you begin to gain an understanding of someone and their
potential, don't stop there! It's important to ask questions from a place
of service rather than from a need to control, manipulate, or force a
particular outcome. But recognize that most questions are opinions
disguised as questions. For example, my friend's mother-in-law often
asks her, "So are you still cooking vegan meals?" What she infers is,
"Your cooking choices are impacting my grandsons negatively. I don't

think they are getting enough protein." Inevitably, that same evening, the subject of protein comes up with a blaming finger pointed at the vegan chef.

Observe yourself when asking questions. Are you in a state of genuine curiosity and seeking to serve, or do you want to judge and prove you are right? Is your mind taking any opportunity to use questions to make itself superior and get its way? Don't let it. Acknowledge the ego at play and let your mind rest. Open your heart to another person with questions founded in openness and love.

What type of questions are best to influence and inspire? I look back fondly at a relationship I had with a man who always asked profound questions of people. Sometimes people were very grateful for being asked. Other times, I noticed that people were uncomfortable to be asked to search for truth, so they brushed the question off. It's fair to say that most of us are masters at running from an examination of truth. I appreciated that this man was not uncomfortable with their discomfort. He simply and gently repeated the question in another way to give the person a second opportunity to look within.

Influencers ask open-ended questions. In fact, influencers usually ask more questions than answers. Trained coaches also ask their clients many questions as they know that the most powerful and lasting change is what happens after people look within and act upon what they see.

SHARE WHAT YOU SEE

When you interact with your team and your colleagues, be observant. When does someone become passionate and excited? Share your observations about the passion and purpose that you observe. This sort of exchange eventually gets to the heart of purpose, because where passion lives, purpose is nearby. At first, this can seem like an awkward conversation to begin with. After all, most of us grew up glossing over uncomfortable conversations, particularly with people who weren't close friends. But as an influencer, you are not here to play small or to skim the surface of life. Your destiny is to influence. Embrace big conversations.

INVITE CONVERSATIONS

Beyond seeing another's calling, invite people into conversations about purpose. Some people light up when they are seen by others and immediately take action toward fulfilling their potential. Others need more time to explore their purpose in conversation with a mentor or with a group that's willing to go deep. Explorations of purpose often contain elements of philosophy, spirituality, science, and the study of motivation. There were "philosophers' cafés" sprouting up seemingly everywhere near my home in past years. People have a need and desire to discuss topics of a grand nature that apply to the most important decisions personally and for the planet.

These types of conversations require a different viewpoint. Influencers who help move the world to a better place see through the eyes of love, not fear. They see what others cannot. They serve as messengers of the Divine. Sometimes, that message needs to be delivered several times in different ways, since people have filters that block them from receiving the information necessary to move forward. An influential leader needs a degree of patience with people's very human reactions of resistance, denial, and procrastination. As influential leaders, however, it's not up to us to ensure they act on what they hear. It's only up to us to deliver the message in a way they can hear it. If we set people up to feel disappointed that they didn't please us, we will, in the end, have little influence. People-pleasing is based in fear, and fear doesn't lead to sustainable change.

MENTOR TO EXCELLENCE

Mentor your team to excellence through Taoist teachings about the nature of the mind and thinking, such as surrender and the mind's need to control and be right. Whenever possible, gently point out thinking patterns that hold them back. These can be as small as someone commenting on poor weather—or any weather for that matter. When people talk about the weather, they usually polarize their experiences into good/bad instead of accepting what is.

Have regular discussions with family and colleagues about topics like acceptance, letting go, compassion, forgiveness, and the need to control and be right. One of my friends has a weekly Friday potluck at work where everyone has the opportunity to lead the discussion around topics such as these. It evolved into a day that everyone looked forward to. It created community. People saw each other as more than colleagues fulfilling a role; they became family who cared for each other.

SUPPORT THE "LEARN WHAT YOU KNOW" PRINCIPLE

As your team, family and group of friends grow in connection, it's important to honor that many topics will need to be addressed more than once. When new perspectives are brought to topics over time, it becomes clearer that there are different ways of seeing the same thing. It encourages an expansion of ideas, open minds, and empathy. It prevents organizations and communities from stunting their growth and getting set in their ways.

When I was in Assisi, Italy, I met Claude Diolosa, a renowned teacher of Chinese medicine, who also facilitates Tibetan meditation. In one of our conversations, Claude told me that he discovered in his Tibetan teachings that it was more helpful to learn what he already knew than to search for more of what he didn't know. That is what has made him

a master of Chinese medicine. He is continually learning about what
he already knows. It may seem paradoxical, but Claude says that each
time he looks at the same information, he gleans new insights and new
ways of expressing the wisdom and teachings.

I have also found this to be true. When I open my mind to curiously
exploring what I already know, I inevitably find great pleasure in
discovering something new. I've found people who get stuck in
relationships or careers most often have a set belief that what they
know is the truth. It prevents them from growing and moving forward.
They're comfortable seeking out what they think they don't know, but
they aren't willing to entertain the possibility of adding to or changing
what they already know. This has caused some companies to shut
down (for example, Kodak failed to acknowledge the importance of
the digital age), marriages to break apart, and countries to suffer from
outdated policies that no longer serve the people.

DEMONSTRATE LEADERSHIP

The final principle of lasting influence is to influence others to lead.
When a leader sees people for who they are, has conversations about
purpose, and supports commitment to that purpose, the mentee is in a
position to listen to ideas about leadership and what it means to lead.
Without clarity and alignment with their soul's calling, it is difficult to
expect people to lead. They may be "natural-born leaders," but their
leadership will be short-lived if they sink into depression or take stress
leave. The need to fulfill one's purpose is the foundation that paves a
path to effective leadership.

Once this foundation is set, begin to demonstrate the principles of
the Tao that lead to effective leadership. Talk openly about your own
challenges in leadership and how you handled those challenges over
time. Share what you learned instead of who made a mistake or who

was at fault. Your stories and experiences will teach better than any information you can offer.

When we mentor up-and-coming leaders, we come across people who have different motives for advancing and fulfilling their personal dreams. Their will may have gotten them to where they are, yet you can invite them to revisit the concept of will. When one's will is grounded in a clear purpose and passion, it can support the creation of a masterpiece. But when it is layered or masked with fears and beliefs of not being enough, the foundation of will crumbles; it cannot sustain itself. People end up sick or too tired to go on. They might even contract an illness or create chaos in the lives of those around them to avoid confronting the brilliance they came here to express.

If that's you, how do you get back to your original state of love-power and begin creating your masterpiece? Start by stripping away all that does not belong to you. Once back to your original state, the "will" to succeed stops being a will. There is no willing—you will act because you are drawn to do so from your greatest source of power: Divine love.

Reflections

Take thirty minutes once a month, scheduled into your calendar, to assess where you are at with the eight elements of creating a purpose-driven team. Rate yourself on a scale of one to ten every month in the eight areas, and make a commitment to work on the one that most needs attention that month. Check in with yourself on the second and third-level purpose that you are embodying and how you might show these levels of purpose more to those around you who are influenced by who you are being in every moment. Celebrate your wins each month with your team and individually. Purpose is one of the few core elements of happy and productive teams and individuals and is the foundation of positive influencers.

Ten

Embracing Divine Purpose

The Sage lives in harmony with all below Heaven.
He sees everything as his own self. He loves
everyone as his own child. All people are drawn to
him. Every eye and ear is turned toward him.

—Tao Te Ching, Verse 49

Third-level purpose is Divine Purpose. It is the fundamental reason for being on the earth. It is the kind of purpose expressed by enlightened beings and spiritual masters; when it is present, it changes all living things for the better.

We all have the same purpose and reason for being here—to love.

When I was going through a challenging time over a decade ago, I was searching for my purpose. I asked for guidance to help me know what I was "to do" with the rest of my life. Every day I would ask this simple question: "What is my purpose?" and every day, I received the same answer: "To love." But instead of accepting it, I was annoyed by it. I wanted career insights! Once I became willing to receive the answer, I began my lifelong quest to be a student and teacher of love.

In that quest, I discovered that we're all students and teachers of love.

While interviewing global influencers for this book, I had the privilege of sharing the stage with Brian Smith, founder of UGG. I was struck by his clear and passionate connection to a greater purpose. When I asked about his connection to purpose, spirituality, and influence, he responded, "I still don't know what my purpose is. I've done good things and built good companies. Every night I close off by saying, 'Thank you, God. It's my will that Yours will be done. Please help me understand Your will.'"

Brian's simple request reminded me that in our daily drive to accomplish and achieve, we often forget that the Greater Will—to love—is always available to us, if we would just be open to receiving and listening.

Brian continued:

> That spirit inside of us knows why we are here. It's got a purpose. Quite often, it's to throw us into circumstances that are completely outside of our control so we can learn perspectives like love and patience—all those great traits that we admire in people. They come from adversity; you are not born with them. You have to learn those things. To have a really powerful spirit does not mean that you are going to have a really easy life. It's probably the opposite. It's going to lead you in directions that are going to be chaos and you are going to have to figure your way out or figure your way through.

As influencers and leaders, we can expect to be continuously challenged in ways that open the door to more compassion, kindness, and love. When we choose to walk through that door, we rise to third-level purpose and become influencers.

When I finally accepted my purpose to love, I noticed that the more I opened to love, the more my purpose focused on serving others. The more I served others from a place of pure love, the more I transitioned into a powerful influencer. When I became present to loving others and to being in a state of love while doing daily tasks, the more clarity I received on steps that would fulfill my second-level purpose. The greatest clarity happens when we are imbued with the peace and joy that love brings. We see what is vital and what is not; we see what we must act on and what can wait. The challenge is to develop third-level purpose in a largely first-level purpose world.

Getting to Third-Level Purpose in a First-Level Purpose World

There are many opinions about what love is, but defining it remains elusive. It's more than being kind, more than loving acts, more than mystical experiences, more than what is left when the mind is not actively thinking, more than the absence of fear. Lao Tzu wisely wrote that "the Tao that can be named is not the Tao," for in naming it, we attempt to control and put boundaries of identity around it. And yet, if we are to explore our purpose "to love," it is helpful to know if we are consistently moving toward fulfilling that purpose.

One way to know we are stepping into third-level purpose is by regularly tending to our power patterns so that we stay in pure love-power as much as possible. If all we did was work with these patterns, we would be on the way to living in third-level purpose. But because many people like to know how to recognize if they are on track to fulfill their purpose to love, I like to point out four qualities that, when they begin to emerge, are clear indicators that you are well on your way to embodying your third-level purpose. They are: openness, joy, peace, and awe.

OPENNESS

Love is vulnerable, curious, and exploratory. Imagine how open you would be to hear what someone else has to say, to consider another perspective, to see the gift others bring to our world when you live without fear or power patterns. Imagine how you would be able to act but not react, how you would try new things, make positive change in your life, and say what needs to be said in the spirit of truth and compassion. Imagine how connected you would feel to others if you didn't have any fear of being rejected or hurt.

All of the business leaders I interviewed had an openness to others and the ability to love others for who they are—not for who society hopes they would be. David Wolfe, superfood and nutrition wizard, noted that he loves everyone, and because of that, he really listens to what they say. When they suggest that he read a certain book or try a certain product, he most often takes them up on the suggestion. He says that the result of being open to others is that synchronicity and guidance become an everyday experience.

David is led to places around the globe, creates products and movements, and shares messages, all because he is open—and not just to people. He is open to nature and how it is constantly guiding and sending us messages. He is open to what he calls the Holy Flow of Life: the mystical force that guides and supports all of us if we are open to receiving it.

Satyen Raja also talks about how being exposed to his parents' openness to their community led to magical experiences in his life:

> If there was an Indian family coming from India and settling into Canada, our house would be the landing portal, where they would set themselves up, get themselves grounded for a month or two, find a job, and then go. So it was a 'Come here, get settled, get yourself together, and go!' kind of support that my parents gave. And so, I was always around new people. And they would always have gatherings,

and food, and parties, and I realized that there's a magic that happens in community that you just can't have if you're with just one or two or a few people. And that there was a magic—a profound magic—that happened in that community. Where there's no teaching, no training, no philosophy, just people sitting around in proximity with each other, breaking bread, telling jokes, grumbling...whatever they need to do with each other—the proximity of beings just being with each other had its inherent profound magic. Where nothing was happening! People are laughing, talking, talking about movies, what they saw... It didn't matter! The content was secondary to the contact! Many times, I thought 'Is it the content?' and I've realized that the content is all secondary, tertiary. What was more valuable, as influence and in the context of influence, and the context of community, was the quality of contact. The openness, the truth, the vulnerability, the joy, the exchange of being to being—as we are right now. The quality of contact.

Satyen's beautiful description of "beings just being with each other" is an invitation for all of us to open ourselves to the powerful experience of pure connection. Technology has in some ways increased openness by making more forms of expression available at our fingertips, but it has also been the excuse for many of us not to connect in person and to establish quality contact. There is truth and beauty in meeting and talking to all people face to face, heart to heart.

JOY

In *Power vs. Force*, Dr. David Hawkins notes that joy, as a form of love, calibrates even higher in energy measurement than love itself:

As love becomes more and more unconditional, it begins to be experienced as inner Joy. This isn't the sudden joy of a pleasurable turn of events; it's a constant accompaniment to all activities. Joy arises from within each moment of existence, rather than any other source.

I have great reverence and awe for joy, and I believe it can perform miracles for ourselves and others. However, I didn't understand *why* I

had this knowing; I just trusted it. When I came across Dr. Hawkins'
work, my knowing was validated by his research. He writes that
individuals who have reached a consistent state of joy (calibrating at
over five hundred) see everything as an expression of love and divinity:

> Individual will merges with divine will. A Presence is felt whose power
> facilitates phenomena outside of conventional expectations of reality,
> termed miraculous by the ordinary observer. These phenomena
> represent the power of the energy field, not of the individual.

The energy field Hawkins speaks of is that universal field from which
we are all born and to which we all return. However, some people are
able to merge with the field consistently, thereby merging with what
many would call an "unusual presence." People often report seeing
light surrounding these highly conscious beings and witnessing light
streaming from their hands. It is no coincidence that many saints are
depicted with halos and streams of light, just as Jesus is often depicted
with light streaming from his heart.

What is also fascinating about the power of joy, according to Hawkins'
research, is that "special" love no longer exists. In its stead, the ability
to love many people simultaneously unfolds. I remember focusing
on meditation and healing practices while I was in the final stages of
divorce, and it gave me space to experience joy once again. At long
last, I was able to recapture the pure joy I had felt as a young girl
who accepted and loved all people. It was the first time I experienced
holding no one as greater or lesser than anyone else, and I felt blessed
to love each person I encountered. While very few people maintain a
consistent state of joy, I believe it is vital that we continuously return
to joy. The more we choose to release power patterns and illuminate
our love-power, and the more we replace our ego's needs and demands
with high vibration behaviors, thoughts, and words, the more we walk
the Tao of Influence and become planetary change-makers.

PEACE

You know it when it's there. It may be fleeting, but you cherish the moments that you feel it and sense it. It feels like the calmness of love. To have peace radiate from your very being, the first step is to examine the way you perceive events and people in the external world. Do you give meaning to what people say? Does that disturb your stillness? Can you see that your own perception of reality is responsible for your lack of peace? If you do, and you continue to work on dismantling the power patterns that keep you stuck in chaos, you will begin to experience more calm and stillness.

The next level of peace is when your internal world and the external world unite, and there is no longer duality; there's no longer a need to label people, actions, or things in categories; there's no longer a need to judge. The outer world becomes part of your inner heaven. I believe there is heaven on earth, but most people cannot experience it because their outer and inner worlds don't align. If you want to be an influencer, you need to inhabit a state of peace that is so powerful it supports others to feel safe and less fearful. From that level of safety, they can make more informed choices. Your presence can do that in their world. In fact, just one master's peaceful presence can be the tipping point between violence breaking out or a return to peace and stillness.

AWE

For many years, I resisted writing about awe as a form of love because I couldn't arrive at an intellectual argument that would support it—that is, until I took a trip to Peru, and my life changed forever. Shortly after my arrival, I was excited to see the sacred site of Machu Picchu, one of the seven wonders of the world. I was determined to absorb every word the tour guide shared as we climbed the seemingly limitless steps toward the site. I could see nothing except the stone beneath my feet, a few brave flowering plants, and many heavily breathing, excited tourists. Suddenly, the tour guide told us to close our eyes and take a few steps forward. Upon opening my eyes, I experienced what seemed like a magical creation out of a Harry Potter book. Every picture and every word I had read about Machu Picchu fell to the wayside as I was completely and utterly awestruck by its beauty.

What impacted me further was that I instantly felt the power of the land flow through my body and radiate out of my hands. My body shook, and I wept tears that only arrive when a wave of Divine energy flows through me. After that experience, I recognized that my receptivity to feeling the experience and being fully present to it allowed me to access pure awe.

For me, awe is a sacred and direct remembering of the Divine within and around us. Awe is the capacity to receive the Divine in all of life. People who live in a state of awe are enlightened beings. They do not need anything to access this state because they've already done the work of arriving at their pure love-power. No matter what the environment, they are literally in awe of life itself.

Influencing Others from Third-Level Purpose

To maintain third-level purpose requires vigilance so we don't fall back into old ways of being and reattach to power patterns. It requires us to keep our love vibration high and continuously choose love over fear. It demands that we meet and accept life as it is, including the people in our lives. Only by constantly and consistently choosing third-level purpose in our daily interactions can we have a lasting influence.

When we make a commitment to grow into third-level purpose, we
inspire others to step into their purpose as well. Satyen Raja speaks
eloquently about witnessing and inspiring purpose in others:

> For me the purest most powerful form of influence is knowing, sourcing,
> and assuming that a person has a deep purpose in life. That they have
> something to contribute to the fabric of reality. And I'm speaking to
> the contribution that they have to the fabric of reality. I'm speaking
> to that in them. I'm not speaking to the small personality. Although it
> includes it, I'm not speaking to their sales goals for that week or that
> day, but I include that. I know that by speaking to the core of their
> interconnectedness, their goal, their dharma, as we call it in yoga, their
> real reason, their ultimate, multidimensional reason for being here.
> When I'm attempting to go for that, the channels open to speak to that.
> Intuitions arise in myself, knowingnesses, and my ability to contact and
> see. And them feeling, 'Wow this person sees me.' Those are the most
> memorable exchanges. That's the influence that happens when you're
> not trying to influence.

Satyen understands well that the Tao of Influence happens when we
are not trying to influence. It happens when we see deeply beyond
the fears and facades into the very God-self of others and when we
speak to the Divine potential and Divine gifts in another. That is true
leadership and influence; that is third-level purpose at its best.

Now, more than ever, we see people who have great wealth and
privilege battling depression and apathy. Teenage suicide rates and
self-inflicted violence in children are at an all-time high. When we are
in third-level purpose, people around us feel loved, seen, and heard.
There has never been great change without most people involved
in the change feeling loved, seen, and heard. Again, this may seem
obvious and simple, yet how many companies have employees who
feel this way? How many institutions nurture their clients and their
community in a way that they feel seen and understood?

I don't believe that leaders simply stop caring, or that they were heartless to begin with, only showing their true colors as time goes on. What happens for most of them is that they have not done the work to clear their power patterns, and so, over time, their team feels the impact of it through lack of connection, isolation, poor communication, and feeling as though who they are and what they contribute does not matter. As leaders, when we work through our power patterns, we become fully present and can see the strengths, possibilities, and psychological blocks of another, unfiltered by our own fears. We become so present that we can embrace the potential of another and support them to shine their light in the direction they are meant to go. Imagine how much more energy would be available for leaders to impact their teams and communities if they surrendered and let go of the human needs that feed power patterns. They would have the energy and focused commitment to inspire individuals and communities to create positive change. They would transform every aspect of their relationships and their relationship to life itself.

It took me a long time to realize to what extent my own third-level purpose was being realized when I was fully present to my clients. A few years ago, a young client of mine who was embarking on a career in counseling was participating in one of my advanced speaking programs. At the end of the event, she shared with me that the first time she met me, she "knew" that she would work with me for an extended period. She knew I could hold her through the challenging times. I asked her to share more, and she went on to say that she had witnessed me being fully present to her and the group, holding each person in their highest potential with both the tenderness of a sage and the fierceness of a warrior. It was then that I realized the true power of presence—the power of Love.

The more that I engaged in presence, the more I became known as someone that had "something extra" when it came to training speakers. People called me and my work "powerful," "intuitive," and "transformational," yet the basis of it was that I was becoming more in touch with reality and truth beyond the facades of ego. The more I lost interest in my ego, the more I dropped into the Now and moved beyond the stories of my own fears and the fears of my clients. I listened to the stories people told me about what was preventing them from being their authentic selves on stage, but I did not see their story as a part of them. I began hearing the greater calling within them that would lead them to move beyond their story into inspired action.

Many leaders fear they will lose their edge and won't be successful (in their career, especially) if they practice being present. Yet studies consistently show that these practices not only help improve people's relationships with themselves and others by being more calm, centered, and focused—they also free up the mind to have more space to create in a shorter period. Employees are more productive and happier, and the bottom line improves. It is a win-win for organizations to help their people learn to become present.

Presence also demonstrates the one thing desired more than anything else: unconditional love. Daniel Gutierrez, author of *Radical Mindfulness*, gives a great example of how third-level purpose influences others:

> I was at the White House at a press conference speaking to Vice President Joe Biden. There was an African American lady there, very timid, and wanting to talk to the Vice President, but she couldn't butt her way in to the conversation; when she finally got a moment to speak to Vice President Biden, she was talking to him with her head down. The next moment got me to respect him a lot. He reached over to her, put her face in his hands and said, "You can look at me. What is it that you'd like?" I just thought that act of kindness is not only authentic but influential all at the same time. He was saying, "I'm here for you. I'm listening. Just to you." This was the second most powerful man in the free world, and he was taking time to make sure that he connects with this person one on one.

> He influenced me that day. Look at the influence that he gave himself.
> This act of kindness and great heart. Influence comes with great hearts.
> He was able to see a person for who they are—not a woman or a man
> or black, Hispanic or Asian, but sees the heart, sees the soul. They could
> have been the only two people in the room.
>
> Influence is the result of a person that can love unconditionally and see
> unconditionally and participate unconditionally. And in doing so, moves
> people to greater good.

As you practice presence with processes such as meditation, gratitude, stillness, spaciousness, and awareness of power patterns, invite your colleagues and team to do the same. Guidance to many of these practices can be accessed for free on the internet; many of the videos and audios that are available for a small cost could make the difference for someone struggling to find purpose and to be fulfilled and productive. Large companies like Google have been role models for their use of tools to help their employees be more present, and as a result, more creative, peaceful, joyful, and fulfilled.

As influencers, we consciously choose third-level purpose states like joy and peace and share them with others. Joy produces joy. One genuine smile from a place of joy can inspire someone feeling down and out. One joyful person entering a business meeting can raise spirits or at the very least, produce a smile. Joy can gift others with physical energy, emotional steadiness, and a sense of hope and gratitude. It is one of the greatest powers we have. We can also choose inner peace. In fact, people throughout history follow great masters of peace. They invest money, time, and resources to be in their presence and learn to develop a state of peace and harmony.

A wealthy man in India traveled a long distance to see Mother Teresa, and when he finally was in her presence, he asked, "What can I do to help save the world?" He was looking to be of importance and to be a Savior (his power pattern), even as he wanted to create peace on the planet.

Mother Teresa laughed and said, "Start with your neighbor. Do you know your neighbor?"

Mother Teresa often said, "Do small things with great love." When you are in a state of peace, you see that there is no separation between small acts and big acts. There is no ego involvement, only the higher consciousness of pure love.

When you're in the midst of your third-level purpose, you may worry that your colleagues or clients perceive you as flaky, childish, or immature. In particular, awe is a quality many business people try to suppress or tame. Perhaps you worry that business might suffer if people perceive you as unstable or "different." If you feel this way, I have two words for you: Richard Branson. Without a doubt, Branson is a beautiful example of a business leader who has built his brand (Virgin Group, Ltd.) to become one of the most successful brands in history, all the while being fully in awe and wonder at life. Notice his ability to laugh, use humor, and be playful—qualities that are connected to awe.

Sure, if you fully embrace awe, you might be seen as different. But every world leader who impacted the earth for good was seen as "odd" by many people. Then judgment turned to acceptance. That's because awe is a form of love, and love is where people yearn to be. It is our home. It is infectious, eternal, and unchanging. It is the only force that has ever been responsible for lasting, positive change in the world.

Merging Divine Purpose with Human Passion

While first- and second-level purpose are grounded primarily in our earthly reality, third-level purpose is connected to the Divine and the cosmic love energy that surrounds us and is in us. If we are to participate fully in our purpose, we're required to be both fully human and fully Divine, merging our Divine Purpose with our human passion for change. We are being called to tangibly influence the planet and to fulfill the call of our soul. Andrew Harvey, in *Evolutionary Love Relationships*, writes:

"We are here, not to vanish into the Absolute, as the Eastern traditions tended to claim, nor to be completely material about our lives, as the Western traditions have increasingly celebrated. We are here to marry the paradox of being grounded in a formless, transcendent truth and light while cultivating our unique self and bringing that unique self to its fullest flowering."

When you merge the uniqueness of your soul's calling with Divine Purpose to love unconditionally, you influence from the highest place, and you become a leader who shifts the globe by what you are doing and who you are being.

Reflections

Meditate on your soul's calling and reflect on how it is connected to each level of purpose. Journal about insights gleaned and set aside time each week to create, tweak, and follow through on a concrete plan to amplify your individual purpose. Once a month, do the same for your collective purpose and your third-level purpose to ensure that you are living a balanced and harmonious life that reflects influence at work, in your community, and within. To assist with this process, subscribe to my YouTube channel (Karen McGregor) for free resources.

Pillar IV

Potential

Eleven

The Holy Flow

Tao is limitless, unborn, eternal—it can only be reached through the Hidden Creator. She is the very face of the Absolute. The gate to the source of all things eternal. Listen to Her voice. Hear it echo through creation. Without fail, She reveals her presence. Without fail, She brings us to our own perfection.

—Tao Te Ching, Verse 6

While the idea of "potential" is often defined as how we might express ourselves on the earthly plane, the potential I speak of is different. There is another level of potential that exceeds human form and merges the unknown with the known, matter with energy. In essence, "potential" is our ability to become a master of both worlds: the human and the Divine. When we walk both worlds at the same time, fueled by the power of love, we walk the path of the Tao, and we are in the Holy Flow of Life. It is characterized by surrendering to life, acceptance of what is, and acting on guidance to serve the world.

To develop this Holy Flow, commit to experiencing the first three pillars of the *Tao of Influence*: dissolving power patterns, becoming fully present, and stepping fully into purpose. However, to fully express that which you are—a Divine being in human form—requires a fourth step: connecting with the energy and essence of God.

We crave the connection to all that is Divine because it's our original home, where we all came from, and where we are all headed back to. Yet in our daily lives, in the busy-ness of all that we do for ourselves and others, we miss out on this connection, and the sacred becomes a distant memory. In fact, when you let this connection go, you may find yourself feeling exhausted, disenchanted, and apathetic. Feelings of sadness or even depression can start to settle in. You might not know where it came from, but you may suddenly be gifted with a Divine insight that reminds you of how much you long to be back in the arms of Love. It is the Love that has never left you. The Love that is constant, unchanging, and formless. It is Home. But daily reality seems so distant from the sacred that you dare not entertain what life would be like if you were able to be home.

It is my hope that if you feel this longing, you will use this pillar of potential to experience a daily connection with the Divine and walk both worlds with joy and grace. However, this journey often starts with feelings of frustration and irritation.

Recalibrate Your Expectations

One step you can take to get closer to coming home to the Divine is to examine your expectations of your connection to all that is God. Your mind has created a litany of expectations that might be stopping you from experiencing the Sacred in every moment. Some common expectations are:

"If I am a good person, God will reward me."

"If I talk to God, He/She better respond!"

"God's response needs to be clear and needs to match my personal desires."

"God shouldn't create any unwanted, arduous struggles."

Can you see how ridiculous these are? And yet every person has personal agendas that they bring to the Divine Table. So, to begin, abandon expectations of what the Divine should look like, act like, or sound like. Dissolve triggers around any word associated with "God," including the word "God." Discomfort with words that name the wordless is an indication that you have not yet experienced the fullness of this Universal Infinite Love, which is beyond any word that can be given.

Once you approach the experience of all that is the Divine with no expectations, as a pure and empty vessel, you begin to discover a deep, authentic, personal connection that changes the fabric of daily reality. You will no longer engage in worldly dramas. People may perceive you as distant or even cold, but this is not the case. You are becoming detached from all that is not God, from all that is not Truth. As a master of both worlds, you merge the human self with the Divine Self and experience life as a joyful journey rather than a never-ending nightmare.

We've already examined the power of meditation to connect with the energy and essence of the Divine. Now it's time to go beyond the twenty-minute, twice-a-day meditation to create a state in which the presence of God is with you always. It's a state where you are aware of the Presence as an infinite support that never leaves you.

Receive Guidance and Support

Before I began helping entrepreneurs share their influential messages on stage, during my years as a trainer of intuition, I developed a process to help seekers become aware of the presence of the Divine. It included training in asking for guidance to serve others and to influence the consciousness of the planet. As wonderful as intuition can be, it can be misused. People frequently begin to use it as a crutch rather than a powerful, sacred support. Some rely on intuition to numb their insecurities around not knowing outcomes of events or ignore their intuition when it does come through clearly. This pattern runs many people's lives; the rest give up, deciding that intuition is fluff and they don't want to engage in it any longer.

When our insecurities run our minds, we ask questions like, "Is this the right man or woman for me?" "Should I leave this relationship?" "Should I make that investment or stick with what I have?" "Will I receive the abundance I've been working toward in the near future?" These are common questions when embarking on a conversation with the Divine, but here's the problem with this approach: when we ask the Divine to give us an answer to something that needs to be addressed through our own dispelling of fears, through our own resistance to change, and through our own dissolving of power patterns, then the answers we receive will always elude and frustrate us. We will never feel grounded by the support we're given because we haven't dealt with the resistance to accepting and acting on the communication given.

Embrace Holy Conversations

The good news is that once we admit we have an agenda with God, are clear on what that agenda entails, and work on releasing it and all expectations that come with it, there are some very concrete ways to experience connection to the Divine. One of these ways is to embrace the Holy Conversation.

The idea of talking to God is a difficult task to wrap our minds around, especially when we are aware of how expansive the Divine is. But you are not going to involve the mind in listening to and talking to God. Sure, your mind will try to control the experience. But as it does, simply release the thoughts as they try to interrupt your experience. The mind will often be successful, of course. Just keep relaxing and releasing the thoughts, including self-judgment around success with this process. The greatest challenge for people beginning this journey is that they cannot differentiate between the mind's will and the conversation and connection with the Divine. Because they lack discernment and trust in the Holy Conversation, they don't act on the wisdom being presented and often address the same issue over and over, hoping for a different answer. Sound familiar?

Once we stop paying attention to the mind's endless and chaotic meanderings and dramas, and lean into another voice, the Voice of Truth, we stop doubting. In a Holy Conversation, you are both the listener and the one who is talking; the Divine is both the receiver and the giver of communication. The key to this exchange is to remember the Sacred Law of Silence: the less words, the better. The less our mind is activated to search for words, thereby searching for new worries, new dramas, and agitating memories, the more space you make for truth to emerge.

With that in mind, learn to ask a simple question that is rooted in love, not fear. You'll know the difference by observing how you feel when you ask the question. If you feel anxious at all, your question is rooted in fear. If you feel a sense of peace or joy, you are vibrating at the frequency of love and are primed for a Holy Conversation. As soon as you ask the question, Truth is revealed. In fact, a response is often given before you finish asking the question.

When Truth is shared with you in this Holy Conversation, you sit in the stillness and notice that the One who is sharing is both speedy and concise. One or two statements is typically all you will receive, most often sounding like the voice inside your head. The statements are not filled with exotic stories and delicious dramas that feed your

fears. Rather, they are matter-of-fact and solid. Boom. There it is. Use
it or choose to bypass the wisdom—it's up to you. You may be given
wisdom or guidance such as, "Have patience." "Leave now." "Eat
better." "Talk to that woman." "Love him." "Let Go."

The *Tao Te Ching* reminds us that, "One who lives in accordance
with nature does not go against the way of things." Yet many of us
choose to ignore the wisdom we receive because we can't muster up
the courage to initiate the change. Yet intuition, by its nature, is going
to demand change. We may see the change as a frightening path into
the unknown, but Guidance will always lead us into personal growth
experiences which impact our role as influencers. Caroline Myss,
author of *Anatomy of the Spirit,* says intuition is energetic data ripe
with the potential to influence the rest of the world. Many people
sense this to be true and keep coming back to the Holy Conversation,
seeking to be altered, yet resisting it at the same time.

Overcoming resistance is also connected to the courage and
willingness to fail, which we are unlikely to entertain because it opens
the deep-seated, original suspicion of being inadequate, unworthy or
unlovable. That's why it's critical to begin working on personal power
patterns and staying present before initiating Holy Conversations.
Otherwise, the mind highjacks the conversation and demands to be
fed an answer that is comfortable, sensible, and void of courage to
do things differently. Do not let it. You now know that it is simply
attempting to protect you, but you were not designed to stay safe.
You were designed to love. Being the expression of love is a mission
that will be anything but comfortable and steady. It is the medicine of
the enlightened.

Every so often, the voice of the Divine may not sound like the voice
you've grown accustomed to. The conversation might not feel like
your usual Holy Conversation; it may feel aggressive or chatty or
even rude. This can happen and will likely happen in situations where
you've become stubbornly attached to the outcomes you desire,

thereby unconsciously drawing in the energies that feed your fear of change and of being present in the Holy Flow.

We live in a universe with many forms of energy that we cannot see and barely understand, and not all possess positive intent for our soul's growth. It is highly possible that the energy form that's talking wants to deliver messages that are not in the Love frequency, bringing us back to outdated power patterns and dysfunctional needs. In most cases, you'll need to command the energy to leave and then immediately feel it or see it leaving your body and energy field. The entire process is quick and painless, but it is important to do when you realize that your Holy Conversation has an unwanted guest. If you feel these steps aren't sufficient to deal with the energy presenting itself to you, ask for support from a trained energy worker to clear and clean up anything that is disturbing your field.

The Holy Conversation is not a private conversation; it is a public awakening of the soul to service. When your heart is wide open and your mind has been trained to take a back seat to this holy exchange, your body will be fully activated to acknowledge Truth. This is a universal law.

See into the Holy Conversation

God is in your blood. In your cells. There is no part of you that is incapable of connecting with this powerful, unimaginable force of Love. And yet, the grand suspicion we collectively hold is that we are distant from God, that only certain individuals have the power, talent, or luck to be able to hear, see, and know the Divine. It's similar to a cultural belief that only certain people can sing, and that these "singers" are the only ones who deserve to sing, contributing to a culture of suppression of our authentic voices. As a result, many have distanced themselves from experiencing the magnificent, soulful power of music by not giving themselves permission to sing anywhere, anytime. And so it is with our relationship with God. The belief that we cannot connect to the Divine stops our senses from experiencing the Holy Conversation. Combined with our original wound of not feeling good enough, it is a perfect recipe for the mistaken perception that we are alone and there is nothing "out there."

Having the awareness of this collective myth, our work is to unravel the illusion and keep coming back to the Holy Conversation with the intention to do what is as natural as breathing: talking and listening to the Divine. With practice, we can experience communication through images as well. These images may come as vague color impressions and then develop into more crystalized visions that, like dreams, are largely metaphorical. Sometimes, the metaphor is explained in the Holy Conversation, but often, it's left for us to unravel as part of our learning journey. Trust that what you see is unearthing your Divine Path and that each vision is connected to your purpose. Treat each vision as Sacred Communication. If you dismiss it as unimportant, you may be neglecting what's most needed to progress as a conscious being with the ability to serve and influence humanity.

Often the vision doesn't immediately come as a picture in the mind. It takes a few moments or even a few minutes to develop fully. The vision can be a still image or, like a dream, encompass movement and sensations. While the vision is unfolding, relax into it and allow it to be what it is without grabbing onto an element of the vision and commanding the mind to make meaning of it. There will be plenty of time afterward to ask about its significance. Notice, I said ask—this is a Holy Conversation, not the monologue of a chaotic mind.

It's helpful to remember to not be afraid of these images. They are mostly metaphorical. For several years along my spiritual journey, I would see an angel presenting me with a gift of a machine gun. Each time I received the gift, I'd ask, "What is this about?" The response was always the same: "Bury this gun and end the war within." To this day,

I feel deep emotion when sharing this vision because by honoring and acting on guidance, all of us can influence world change and become what spiritual teacher Andrew Harvey called, "Sacred Activists." We can serve others and take on the enormous challenges of the planet while continually developing our connection to the Divine and releasing all that is not love.

At some point in the Holy Conversation, ego will attempt to tamper with the vision. This happens when the vision is being forced into existence. Surrender to the vision guiding you; don't try to guide it. (This advice is especially useful for Controllers.) When desire for clarity takes over, we make something up. Don't allow your needs to dominate the Holy Flow of this conversation. If the conversation is brief and your human expectations are not satisfied with it, or if the conversation is vague and you struggle to gain clarity, simply disengage and ask the question, "What is it that I am to learn from this?" If you ask with an open heart and have a willingness to act on the answer, you'll receive clarity. It may not be the clarity you want, but it is the clarity you most likely need in the moment.

Feel into the Holy Conversation

Opening up to hearing and seeing the Holy Conversation is one of the most beautiful journeys I've experienced. The experience reminds me that I'm never alone and that humanity is supported in the most exquisite ways that the mind cannot comprehend. What looks like devastation may indeed be the greatest stepping stone to becoming the influencer you want to be. Your best opportunity to serve and to make real and lasting change is by using your setbacks and traumatic events as a form of guidance. As difficult as it is for the mind to hear this, nothing that happens to you is designed to hold you back and make you suffer; it is designed to birth a new movement, a new message, and a new planet sustained by love. More than ever before, mystics are coming out of their monasteries, businesses, homes, and shelters. They are feeding the planet with actions of love and supporting the vision for a new world with sacred activism.

As our bodies begin to feel more, our minds want to make meaning of the feelings because that is what we have done our entire lives. Notice that the feelings you feel in the Holy Conversation are not emotions, they are the signature of God written on your body. They may bring forth an urge to yawn and release energy. They may be a feeling of joy that floods your heart and delivers Truth tears. They may arrive in the form of tingles over certain parts of your body. They may present themselves as heat or cool air blowing across your body. Or they may be an indescribable knowing that some people call a "gut feeling." All these sensations, and more, are part of the Holy Conversation. They will become a daily reality as your heart opens to connecting with the Divine. If you allow yourself to act on the support and guidance given in the Holy Conversation, your service to the world will be exponential, and the love that your service imbues will be the greatest source of influence.

When I interviewed Brian Smith, I saw how a powerful brand (UGG) was built by a man who allowed himself to feel the Holy Conversation and be guided by it. Brian shares,

> There is a powerful spirit inside me that everyone has. This force or being inside me, if I slowed down or listened to it, would guide me, often in the form of goosebumps. I'd be thinking on a problem and suddenly I'd have some thought and I'd immediately erupt in goosebumps. That I've come to learn is my Inner Spirit saying, 'Yes Brian go for it. You are on the right track.'
>
> Each time I hit the wall or got depressed because of things happening in my business, it was usually because I hadn't slowed down and meditated for a week or two. At some point, I'd say, 'Brian just slow down and give it up' and I'd start meditating again. And amazingly

the direction came from inside. It wasn't like I thought about it intellectually. A feeling came over me that 'this is the right direction and keep going.' And that Inner Spirit has guided me not just through the UGG business, but it's guided me still to this day.

Brian's trust and ability to receive a Holy Conversation allowed him to access the abundant gifts of the Universe and, in so doing, help many others along the way.

Focus on the Greater Good

As you become more confident in your journey with the Holy Conversation, as you work through Power Patterns and ego needs, your personal desires and individual goals lessen. The Conversation will turn to your soul's greater purpose and desire to be a vessel for what wants to come through you. It will be evident that you exist for reasons beyond getting through your own troubles and reaching personal milestones. At this point, the Holy Conversation will guide you into actions that uplift humanity, and you will have the strength and courage to take steps to facilitate the unfolding of the greater good. This is where true Leadership begins. This is the heart of all Influence.

Reflections

Take some time to journal about your agenda with God. What are your expectations, fears, and needs? What power patterns do you engage with the Divine? How are they blocking the Holy Conversation? Why do you doubt the action you are being asked to take? Be as raw and honest with yourself as possible; the truth may surprise you, but it is the doorway to growth.

Practice initiating Holy Conversations several times a day—as you wake up, before you go to sleep and, ideally, following your meditation practice. Notice your thoughts and emotional state immediately before entering the conversation. If it is ungrounded, chaotic, or lacks a sense of peace, use practices like grounding, deep breathing, and visualizing to assist you in releasing the stressful thoughts. Record the guidance you receive as well as the resistance and fears that arise in you from the guidance. You are well on your journey as an influencer.

Twelve

Mastery in Form

*The Great Perfection seems imperfect; yet this world
it creates is never impaired. The Great Fullness seems
empty; yet this world it creates is never lacking.*

—Tao Te Ching, Verse 45

The Holy Conversation invites us into our purpose to serve and to love in both the physical and non-physical worlds. What you do on a daily basis to initiate the Holy Flow and to master both worlds involves more than accessing higher realms and working through power patterns. It also involves placing your learnings and integration of learnings into form. When you commit to mastery of form, or mastery of your creations, you become a true influencer.

Mastery requires commitment to the highest level of creation possible. It is derived from our pure love source. When in a state of unconditional love for ourselves and others, we ignite all levels of purpose to create something masterful. It is not based in ego or trying to be the best or trying to outsmart someone else. It's based on a call to serve the world through the energy of love.

Mastery is also a commitment to the unknown potential within. It requires trust that we are unlimited souls, capable of creating things we can't envision yet. Mastery is the gateway to infinite possibility. Each time we step toward mastery, we get closer to infinite expansion. Each time we say "Yes" to giving that repetitive task or doing that thing that scares us, we are saying "Yes" to the unknown space within that has more potential to create than we can even comprehend.

Because most people intuitively sense the bigness of their potential, it's critical to be aware of the elements that block mastery. Aside from the fact that most countries and cultures now give little credence to mastery, instead emphasizing efficiency and output, we can *all* move toward it. To do that, let's first look at common assumptions and perspectives on mastery that inhibit its natural unfolding.

The Myths of Mastery

Many people I meet who are entering a new career believe that mastery requires perfection, and so feel that it is to be feared or avoided. Unfortunately, one of the downsides of our exposure to personal development is the perception of perfection. Aiming for something we can never achieve—perfection—we think there's a connection between our pursuit for perfection and the reason we don't love ourselves.

I am a big believer in the idea that human beings—if unhampered by fear and inherited belief systems—are inspired by perfection and yearn for it. It's not the type of perfection that feeds off beliefs such as "I'll never be good enough"—it is the type of perfection that unfolds when creating at an exceedingly high level. When you have used your gifts, skills, focus, and determination, combined with a great love for what you do and who you serve, you will always have a healthy respect for reaching the highest level possible in your field—what I call *perfection*. In fact, if your body and heart remain open, you will naturally gravitate toward perfection.

It is only when we fall for the idea that we are not good enough that we run from perfection or push it away. Have you ever witnessed someone who is tremendously talented yet won't put the required energy and effort into their craft to get to a level of mastery? Although they have purpose and passion, their fear of perfection (which is really a fear of not being good enough) stops them from ever trying. Don't let this happen to you. Be aware of your ego's needs and the power patterns these needs feed into. Be vigilant of the mind's agenda to limit you. You are free to walk away from the fear and illusion that you were not meant for perfection. If the universe is perfection—and you are part of it, after all—then you will inherently reach for perfection with love and joy.

People mistakenly believe that perfection means there is no room left for potential. If we look at Michelangelo, who invested three years of his life, day and night, creating the sculpture *David*, we admire his tenacity to create such a beautiful work of perfection. Millions of people stream into Florence, Italy, every year to behold the magnificence of the sculpture, which the Italians lovingly refer to as "The Giant." Michelangelo was only twenty-six when he created David. He did not stop just because people deemed the work to be perfect in every way. He did not let that hamper his great love for sculpting. Instead, he went on to create many more astounding works, tapping into the infinite potential within his mind, body, and spirit. Michelangelo was fascinated with aligning his work with God and was deeply in touch with the Holy Conversation. He had a firm belief that he was the vessel through which the Divine created beautiful works of art.

Another assumption about mastery that hampers many people from tapping into their potential is that people must be ultra-gifted and show enormous potential from the beginning, or it's not worth even trying. We don't have to look very far to see the flawed thinking in this. Michael Jordan, one of the greatest basketball players in history,

did not make the tryouts for his high school basketball team. Gymnast
Mary Lou Retton, when she was competing in the 1984 Summer
Olympics, was not expected to receive medals, much less the five she
went home with. After having been rejected by twelve publishers,
J.K. Rowling's first book was accepted by a small publishing house
only because the publisher's eight-year-old daughter loved it. The
publisher told Rowling to get a job because she would not make any
money writing children's books. J.K. Rowling became the first female
billionaire author. Her beloved Harry Potter series became the number
one bestselling series of children's books of all time.

The myth that giftedness is a requirement of mastery also shows up
in business. Many business owners close their doors, believing that
the challenges encountered are proof that they are not capable of nor
sufficiently gifted to run a successful business. When I interviewed
Brian Smith, he shared the story of the tremendous struggles he
experienced getting UGG off the ground. Several times in his early
years of building the company, he thought that he would have to shut
it down due to lack of profitability. Brian shared one critical lesson
learned that now serves the many audiences he speaks to:

> You can't give birth to adults. Just like an infant in a cradle can't get up
> and go to college, everything has to go through that infancy. There's not
> a company on the Wall Street Journal's stock exchange page that didn't
> start out in infancy. Knowing that they can go from infancy to toddler to
> youth to teenager to adult gives them peace of mind that where they
> are now is the right place to be.

Brian's wisdom reminds me that mastery is the work of an elder,
not an infant. But to be the elder, you need to experience growing
phases first.

In North America, there is also a strong assumption that mastery is the
work of genius in isolation. People believe that others are only able to
achieve great mastery because they spend inordinate amounts of time

alone to focus and get to a new level of excellence. Sadly, isolation is the norm in North America, but it isn't in other parts of the world, nor has it been that way throughout history.

This became evident when I traveled to Italy and learned about the Renaissance artists, the majority of whom were born and raised in Florence, which had a population of 70,000 at the time. How could such a small population produce so many of history's greatest artists in a fifty-year time frame? To find the answer, I looked no further than the daily actions of Renaissance kids native to Florence. As teenagers, the great Renaissance artists spent months at a time studying just one great work of art, drawing, or painting it over and over, conversing with their friends about the art and their own art and then showing the progress they were making to the maestro. Perfection existed within a supportive environment of like-minded, inspired people.

We like to think of perfection as something that mysteriously sprouts up in genius hermits, but it's not true. It grows in community and within the constructs of a carefully nurtured environment. Leonardo Da Vinci was said to have spent an additional ten years working with his maestro and alongside up-and-coming artists, even though he had already become well-known for his art.

Another inspiring and more recent example of mastery in the field of speaking and training is Tony Robbins. Many people wonder how he became a celebrity icon in the personal development arena. Like many stars, Tony was inspired to support people to make change, but he was also willing to go beyond what most people are willing to do. He spoke far more than the average speaker and trainer: three times per day in his early years! He got feedback constantly about his speaking—every day in fact! Imagine how good you would become if you spoke three times per day to audiences of all types and sizes!

As an entrepreneur who has mastered creating and delivering powerful talks, I am convinced that the more isolated people become, the less likely they are to develop mastery in their craft. When people create in isolation, they tend to be more sensitive to feedback and avoid looking at other people's masterpieces. The high-level works of other people bring inspiration and energy to the solo creator, who gets to experience new ideas and tweak those needing a facelift. The process becomes the feeding ground for a new level of mastery.

Commitment

Commitment can also help free us from resistance to our path and goals. Satyen Raja talks about the evolution of choice and how he has managed to stay committed to practicing the highly challenging art form of Brazilian jujitsu:

> When I'm not feeling well, or overwhelmed, or exhausted, seven out of ten times I don't want to go to class. Because it's tough. But it gets easier and easier. It's interesting, one of my teachers in class—whenever I mention, 'Oh yeah, it's a tough day I'm exhausted...'—says, 'Don't worry, we're going to take it easier today.' It's never the case. It's harder than I could ever imagine! But his tone sounds like it's going to be the easiest class in the world. But what he actually puts me through is just as hard as anything else, if not harder! Always! So now I've come to the place where it's my choice that takes me to class, and he's helped me ground in the choice that takes me to my class rather than my emotional state or my feeling of readiness or willingness. It has nothing to do now with my choice of going to class and developing myself. It's simply my choice itself. To show up.

Take time now to reflect on key areas of life: relationships, work, finances, recreation, health, and spirituality. Are you following through on what you most value in each area? Are you taking steps toward your vision in each area? Once we identify the areas that need work, we can make written and verbal commitments to the things we say "Yes" to. Say "Yes" to the choice to show up. Commitment requires a strength of character; it is not for those unprepared to deal with the resistance and challenges that arise. Yet the rewards are a sense of peace, stillness, and happiness that elevate consciousness.

When determining what to say "Yes" to, make a daily or weekly plan of small steps toward your commitment. At first, don't be concerned with a five-year goal or even a one-year goal. Just focus on what you can do today. Today quickly becomes tomorrow, next week, next month, and next year. Soon you'll develop the confidence to know you won't stop or quit, and you'll be able to work with longer time frames.

Another common assumption about mastery is that it unfolds in an environment free of criticism and lavish in praise. With studies showing the positive impact of praising children, it's clearly important to acknowledge what children can do rather than what they can't do yet. When it comes to mastery, however, constructive criticism is vital to advancing skills to a much higher level. Like diamonds, we need to be put under pressure to shine. Most of us never get to mastery because we don't get over the need to be right and the need to control the situation (so that the belief we are not enough is never exposed or felt). Dr. Norman Vincent Peale said, "The trouble with most of us is that we would rather be ruined by praise than saved by criticism." Be open to loving, constructive criticism and challenging questions.

Perfect creations exist within a challenge and thrive in a community of challengers. Some of the greatest companies today have leaders that provide environments of challenge that result in the perfection of products, visionary ideas, and solutions to tough problems. Perfect creations exist in a community that is safe to challenge one another constructively. When it's safe to voice concerns and offer critique, a masterpiece can be birthed.

Soul Transitions and Follow-Through

The years I spent offering workshops centering on soul purpose gave me great insights into the elements vital to mastery. Many people question what they should be doing with their lives, whether they are in the right job, or if they are following their true soul's calling. What sometimes stops them from making the shift (beyond survival fear and power patterns) are the myths they hold about mastery. By holding onto the myths, they stay stuck—unable to make the smallest shift toward what their soul is guiding them to. However, when they do take small steps on the road to mastery and have the courage to take these steps daily, they discover they're bigger than the myth. They're bigger than the illusions they bought into.

One of the common objections to mastery that beginning speakers have is: "I'm too old to do this." They liken creating a powerful talk to climbing Mount Everest with no physical training! And indeed, it can seem overwhelming to the mind—but we are not our minds! We are an infinite source of love energy that is yearning to create and serve the world.

"This is too hard," is another common pushback to one's calling. Clearly, it indicates the person is letting their mind win, as few things are "too hard" for people who've committed to daily habits to master a skill and birth their creation. "I don't have time to master anything," is a comment nursed by our frenetic society, when someone is proudly obsessed with how busy they are. Yet our souls would not be calling us to make a transition and create a new reality that serves the world if we didn't have time for it. The fact is, we choose how to invest our time and what to invest our time in. When we claim full ownership over our time, small changes in our current reality lead to carving out time to begin the journey of mastery. The grit to start and complete a creation was not born of our mind's excuses. Mastery involves the courage to overcome the desire for safety from the known. It acknowledges the

Law of Change and flows like water around objections and fears to its end goal of creation. Mastery is a high form of influence.

Reflections

Journal about your relationship to mastery and perfection. What has held you back from embracing mastery? What views do you have about perfection that might be stopping you from committing to mastery? What is one action that you can take today toward creating a masterpiece or mastering a skillset?

To begin embracing mastery and perfection as a leader, consider taking these three steps:

1. CREATE A CULTURE OF RECOGNITION

Organize regular gatherings at work and at home where gifts and abilities are formally recognized. Say and do things that show and remind others, "I see you. I know your potential." Many great masters have been influenced to create at the highest level simply by someone else seeing what they were capable of.

2. CREATE A CULTURE OF MODELLING AND MENTORSHIP

Nurture passions and talents within yourself and others by introducing the perfection of masters. Study these masters and masterpieces together in groups and have diverse conversations about them. Find a long-term mentor who is a living master of your passion. Da Vinci's success was in large part due to his relationship with his Bottega mentor, Verrocchio.

3. CREATE A CULTURE OF CHALLENGE

Commit to meeting regularly with a handful of brave people who
challenge you just as you challenge them. These are not your
agreeable friends; choose people who are qualified to critique and
have dissenting opinions. Challenge schools and workplaces to adopt
initiatives that give time and space for the mastery of passions. In
its early years, Google found that by having its engineers dedicate
20 percent of their work time toward passion projects, 50 percent of
their best products were created, including Gmail, Google News, and
Google AdSense. Some schools are now adopting a Genius Hour, a
weekly initiative that honors the passions of students and gives them
weeks—versus days or hours—to perfect their projects.

Thirteen

From Mysticism to Activism

Though Tao gives life to all things, Te is what cultivates them. Te is that magic power that raises and rears them, completes and prepares them, comforts and protects them.

—Tao Te Ching, Verse 51

Spiritual teacher Caroline Myss' book, *The Interior Castle,* is based on the original work of saint and mystic Teresa of Avila. In it, Myss describes "mystics out of monasteries"—people who walk both the spiritual world and the human world masterfully. They are the people who have committed their lives to experiencing God in their bones—but that doesn't mean that they are sitting quietly in meditation most of the day. They are offering their mastery, their creations, and their love-power through service to the world. Mother Teresa is a prime example of a mystic who, with ceaseless passion, held the poor and dying, comforted the diseased, and fed the homeless.

It's time to embody both mysticism and activism. While moving through your private journey with the Divine and experiencing love-power arising within yourself, there's a call for your soul to use your gifts, talents, and love for humanity to create real change on the planet. This is the love that drives activism. It is a love that is not only for yourself or for a few select people, but a love for all through consistent action-taking. Bestselling author of *Radical Mindfulness*, Daniel Gutierrez, says, "Don't be so heavenly bound you're no earthly good." It's a great reminder for those times when we feel out of balance: we must apply our spiritual growth to the world we live in *for* the world we live in.

As Daniel notes, if you are going to be a mystic and take action toward a better world, you must "die to the self every day and in every moment." That's why navigating your personal power is so vital: when you feed your ego, you make it stronger, and you become less able to impact the world positively and sustainably. By dying to the ego's needs, obsessions, and preferences, you embody more of the love that you are. You become a true influencer. Daniel says,

> If we come from the standpoint that I am a vessel for the universe to be used for the greater good of mankind, then I am guided. Whether delivering a speech at Carnegie Hall or talking to a homeless person on the street, having that same level of compassion requires that I die to myself every single day, and in every moment, so that the Greater Good can process itself through me.

While speaking about the balance and union of being and doing, Daniel asks us to inquire, "What is the greater good for all?" That's where mysticism and activism come together. We need to have the capacity to connect to the Divine and then others. That is the way to be of utmost service to humankind.

Starting a Movement

One way to lean into activism is to create or join a movement. I had the honor of interviewing an expert in starting and sustaining movements: Joseph Ranseth. He shared that the greatest leaders in history who led movements were also excellent communicators with a powerful message. They knew how to spread messages impactfully. Dr. Martin Luther King, Jr., Jesus, and Mahatma Gandhi are three examples of influencers who shifted the course of humanity. Ranseth pointed out that the difference between these luminaries and the majority of activists nowadays is that they were not using their influence to simply engineer a transaction (a change in outer behavior) but to create transformation (a lasting inner change). When the focus extends beyond transactions and the ego bows down to the work of collective transformation, there is less desire for individual significance. The focus is on service to others rather than service to an individual's desired goal or outcome.

The Role of Passion

To move from mysticism to activism, great passion is required. Most books about passion reference a deep love for our chosen careers or hobbies. While useful to an extent, it's limited in that it bypasses the passion for social justice. Justice—not from the ego's perspective of needing to be viewed as the change-maker—but addressing the injustice of structures designed to keep down those who are suffering and disempowered.

Most people confuse the feeling of anger or rage as a fault or weakness. It is anything but. In our numb world, people have forgotten what it is like to care for those who are powerless and unable to speak for themselves. Many have forgotten what it is like to care about the earth, which is ravaged daily. The lack of care comes from decades of structures and institutions that have told us what to focus on. If we were trained to be more in touch with our hearts and the heart of Mother Earth, if we were surrounded by that which honors the Great Mother and not the things that destroy her, we would pay attention when we lose four acres of Amazon rain forest per minute. We would pay attention when another sea mammal loses its life to indiscriminate use of single-use plastic. We would pay attention to the silence of the suffering amongst the noise of social media.

Our attention wanes in a second, and the powers that be want to keep it that way; rage, an igniter of change, is unwelcome. So "caring" has turned into vanilla comments on social platforms such as Facebook, as in: "Sending you good energy" or adding a heart like a tourist passing through. We go about our day not giving the situation a second thought.

The passion of deeply caring is a great love of humanity. It is rooted in the peace of love, yet it may not appear on the outside as calm and benevolent. Jesus is an example of a man who embodied both mysticism and activism—and he was known to become angry and to say things that provoked crowds. This is what is needed at times to move the world forward in its evolution. Yet observe how often this type of passion is described in the media and by the public as hysterical, uncontrollable, irrational, and moody. The suppression of passion is all around us, yet that passion is the Voice of Truth. And aligning with Truth is the only way sustainable, evolutionary change happens.

It takes great courage to stop buying into the structures that global powers create in their zeal to hide truth. It takes courage, not only to see clearly and unplug, but to help victims of corruption who can't help themselves. When we step into our feelings of anger and rage that ignite our sacred activism, others begin to align with the call for truth and justice. They are encouraged by our courage to make real change happen.

Balance

One of the challenging aspects of balancing mysticism and activism is maintaining a healthy relationship to time. There's a delicate balance between knowing that time is of the essence when it comes to alleviating suffering and unspeakable atrocities on the one hand, and feeling calm, peaceful, and patient with the time we've been given to offer support on the other. By using the tools required to become more present, as outlined in Pillars One and Two, you can feel grounded peace in the Holy Moment of Now. These tools eventually become your state of being and flow into your activist state to merge as a holistic experience. You'll feel the urgency to assist without feeling irritated that things are not happening fast enough. You'll embrace patience while still being fueled by the Divinely-guided message to "Act now." Your Divine and human aspects will intersect and merge together, unfolding your creations and co-creations that shift the world.

Another challenge to remaining balanced revolves around how much time it's best to be in solitude. Once people have let go of personal needs and power patterns, they tend to thrive with varying degrees of solitude. Even with a meditation practice, constantly ruminating on our to-do list with no time to "be" causes a lack of peace, heightened by no delegation or request for support. To experience more solitude, and at the same time, get your movement off the ground, gather a team of dedicated and passionate people who work enthusiastically for the cause.

Joseph Ranseth shares that great leaders who produced massive shifts in consciousness and focused on bringing unity to the planet did so by effectively creating teams of support. Even if they didn't achieve their goals of unity due to mass human ignorance, with the help of others, they shifted perceptions enough to make radical changes. "Gandhi was trying to bring unity between Hindus and Muslims in one nation liberated from British Rule," Ranseth said. "Even though he failed at this ultimate goal, the successful political outcome he did create was a by-product of the change in thinking, which is that 'we are all of equal value.'"

When there is a call to action that is unity-inspired, a core group of people begins to shift, and when they do, the laws of the universe dictate that it isn't long before others follow. But none of this comes to pass without the leader of the movement humbly remaining a mystic within the movement; it activates the right type of support for the movement to thrive.

Support can also come in the form of our beloved. There is no greater calling of a romantic relationship than to create a better world together. Antoine de Saint-Exupery, author of *The Little Prince*, said, "Life has taught us that love does not consist in gazing at each other but in looking outward together in the same direction." Many millennials are moving the world in this direction. Rather than being absorbed by one another, they are now breaking the old paradigm of romantic codependency and choosing instead to be inter-dependent, working together for causes that uplift humanity. This new paradigm of relationship lets people shift from a state of isolation within their own dramas, fears, and wounds, which are experienced as they get to know their partner, to becoming a presence in the world. As such, they are reminded of a truth within the Tao of Influence: our private agonies will always be there waiting for us to tend to, but together, we can be lifted to our higher purpose. High-purpose couples generate a new love and passion within their relationship as they create change that alleviates suffering and brings greater consciousness to the world.

Energy

Modern-day mystics transforming the world through their message and actions require an abundance of energy. As a result, they're dedicated to opening their Shakti, their infinite love-power. Michael Singer speaks at great length in his lectures about the importance of retaining this energy. It is energy that never grows old; it is simply the natural and limitless flow of love-power that comes when our hearts open to life and stay open despite circumstances. Our energy depletes when we close and increases when we open. It is diminished when we step into our power patterns and surges when we choose to release and let go of these patterns. The practice of accepting what is and letting go of what was is vital to movements, because many times, conditions are far from perfect. We can feel discouraged when witnessing injustice, inequality, and pain. No matter what feelings arise, it's vital to keep opening the heart and doing the work to remain in the flow of love-power.

Ranseth says activists need to examine their own attachments and aversions when creating or joining a movement. What are we hanging on to mentally and emotionally that keeps us in lower forms of energy? What are we running away from that results in energy depletion? He asserts,

> You don't burn out when you are peaceful. You burn out when you are in an energetic state where you are compensating for some imbalance or misalignment in your inner world. When we are balanced and living in alignment, it doesn't matter so much how we manage our calendar because we are managing our energy. If we are not managing our energy, then our calendar gets out of balance. We've all had this phenomenon of working extremely long hours without getting tired or burned out, because we're so connected and aligned. We've also had the experience of working far fewer hours and getting totally burned out. And that is because we are out of alignment.

To return to alignment, Ranseth suggests asking yourself, "What is the transformation that I want to see happen in the world, and how am I embodying that transformation right now? What can I do to further embody that transformation?" When tuning in to our inner selves and reflecting on these questions, we can understand what is off-balance and bring it back into balance so that the transformation occurring inside is also occurring outside. Once that happens, and you're opening to the flow of life, energy flows freely and without limit.

Energy is also impacted by the tendency to get overwhelmed by the Big Picture. We feel swamped by the number of things to do and forget that the foundation is in our beingness. Ranseth explains:

> If you want to create a movement, you need to realize that everything you do now is mirroring the bigger outcome you are working toward, whether you like it or not! To obtain maximum impact, ask the question, 'How well do I embody the change I want to see in the world, right here, in me, in my home, in my family, in my community?' Slowly shift the focus outward. Imagine your movement as a series of concentric circles. If you try to focus on an outer ring without first getting a closer one dialed in, you immediately become out of balance and you won't have the impact that you want.

Reflections

Journal about where you are on the continuums of mysticism and activism; personal growth and outward expression of that growth; and of love for self, another, and humanity. Begin to bring awareness to the passion you have for particular injustices and ask, "Who do I have to become to begin to alleviate this problem? What is one small step I can take to help heal this global problem? Who else is passionate about ending suffering and working toward real and lasting change? How can I meet or reconnect with these people?"

Final Thoughts

Have faith. Follow your own shining. Be aware of your own awareness. On the darkest nights you will not stumble. On the brightest days you will not blink. This is called "The Practice of Eternal Light."

—Tao Te Ching, Verse 52

Congratulations for taking this journey and courageously walking the path of the Tao. You've traveled through the muddy terrain of power patterns and the uphill climb of practicing presence. You have taken the rocky journey into different levels of purpose and explored the limitless road of potential—fully seen after completing the four pillars of influence.

It's fair to say that you may stumble on your path as you integrate the four pillars into your day-to-day life. You may even feel stuck for a period of time, particularly as you work through the complexities of your inner being and your relationship to Power, the first pillar of influence. It can be challenging to constantly be aware of thoughts and needs that feed into and shape power patterns. Yet when you understand how your love-power gets distorted by power patterns and use the tools provided here, you engage in "The Practice of Eternal Light" that Lao Tzu refers to in Verse 52 of the Tao Te Ching. This practice leads to great internal freedom, love, joy and positive change for yourself and the planet.

In the journey of Presence, the second Pillar of the Tao, you are invited to be here now and train your mind to work in flow versus resistance.

Once present to life, your mind quiets, and joy and peace grow from fleeting moments to regular states of being.

Now for the third Pillar: Purpose. In this portion of your journey, you not only activate unconditional love, the highest state of the third pillar, but you also become a leader who influences others to align with all levels of their purpose.

Finally, you experience the Tao of Influence as Potential. You merge the Truth that binds heaven and earth, and you become a mystic who learns to use your power to create positive change and to influence others to do the same. You become an influencer through who you are being and through the creations you have made manifest on the planet.

I now invite you to proclaim to yourself and others that you're no longer willing to participate in the daily dramas of humanity. That you are no longer going to believe what they believe, think like they think, or act like they act. You change; then they change. It is the natural flow of the universe. If enough people turn to the possibility of Truth and Love, others will follow. That is the Way of the Tao. Not through force—just by being what you really are.

Transitioning into the Love-Power Paradigm

As you progress on the path of the Tao and your journey as an influencer, it is normal to feel impatient with yourself and your varying states of being. You may feel irritated or tired as you experience changes in yourself. This was my reality a few years ago, after facilitating powerful events back to back. My body felt like it was undergoing a shift that required me to be patient as I endured exhaustion. I was anything but patient.

When I asked my spiritual advisor why this was happening, she told me that as my consciousness and love-power grew, I was also raising the vibration of the rooms in which I spoke to a much higher energetic state. She wisely saw that what I thought was exhaustion was actually the opening of a new love consciousness that was transforming old paradigms. She pointed out that when a new paradigm and an old paradigm meet, there can be resistance that requires a period of adjustment. I needed to simply be in the energy of the two paradigms while also making small choices every day to be aware of the old—but not to go back to the old. Once you see, you cannot un-see. Once you rise into pure love, you cannot dip into familiar power patterns without awareness and consequences.

To hold a high love vibration consistently takes practice. A lifetime of awareness and choices. But I cannot imagine a more necessary and rewarding journey for ourselves, our communities, and our planet.

The Journey of a thousand miles begins
With a single step.

—**Lao Tzu**

P.S.

I invite you to join our community of influencers who care and dare to shift the world in positive new directions. Please join our community on Facebook: Influence and Ancient Wisdom for Inspired Leaders https://www.facebook.com/groups/ InfluenceAncientWisdomInspiredLeaders/ and subscribe to my YouTube channel (Karen McGregor) for videos that further support integration of the concepts in this book.

If you'd like more information on creating a powerful message that influences the world, please visit www.SpeakerSuccessFormula.com.

Also, I would love to hear your stories and insights gleaned from reading this book, and the ways in which you are making shifts in your business, family, and community. Please contact me at www.KarenMcGregor.com to share.

Acknowledgments

There are many people who supported and loved this book from its inception to birth. I have deep thanks for each of you, who are part of my online community, friends, family, and colleagues. You know who you are. Big love to each of you.

Deep thanks to Randy Peyser, my literary agent, who believed in my book and my message with fierce love and a playful heart. Randy was instrumental in my book getting into the hands of so many people who needed to hear the message that influence is a spiritual directive. Thanks to my publishing team at Mango, in particular Brenda Knight, Robin Miller, and Chris McKenney, who believed in my vision of a new kind of leadership and influence.

Profound gratitude for the brilliant wordsmiths that supported me: my first editor, Sylvia Taylor, who was my earth angel, encouraging the message with clarity, direction and loving guidance, Diane Eaton, who made the manuscript sparkle and shine with love, and my publisher's editor: MJ Fievre, who supported the manuscript with insightful feedback that made it's message even more powerful and clear.

A huge hug to all the powerful beings that chose to share their wisdom by being interviewed for *The Tao of Influence*: Mathew Knowles, Satyen Raja, David Wolfe, Michelle Falcone, Daniel Gutierrez, Dr. John Demartini, Brian Smith, Joseph Ranseth and Teresa de Grosbois. Your words remain in my heart and emanate into the world as loving influence.

Deep gratitude to my marketing and PR team, who continue to expand the reach of the book so it is read by the people who are inspired by its message. Deep thank you Mat Miller, Jon James, Catherine

Skaley-Stevens and Dottie DeHart for your support in marketing, PR, and social media love. This book would not be where it is today without you.

Thanks to my beloved family. This book is informed by my loving journey with you: my mom, my first teacher of love, and my sons, Matthew and Mitchell, who teach me daily the Way of the Tao.

A final thank you to the Holy and Sacred One. Infinite gratitude for Stillness of Being.

About the Author

Karen McGregor is a thought leader, global speaker, and catalyst for influencers who have a passion for creating positive change in the world. She supports leaders to become masters of both their internal environments and their external systems and processes, thereby becoming a powerful force for change.

Karen is the founder of Speaker Success Formula, a training company that has supported hundreds of thousands of professionals and entrepreneurs over the past decade to create and deliver powerful messages on stage. She has shared her message on stage with luminaries like Tony Robbins, Deepak Chopra, John Gray, and David Wolfe. Her TEDx talk has been viewed by over one million people and her ideas and direct quotes have been featured on CTV News, *Readers Digest, Breakfast Television* (Toronto, Canada), *USA Today, Florida Weekly*, and many other prominent media outlets.

To learn more about Karen and receive free additional resources on the topic of influence and leadership please visit: www.KarenMcGregor.com.

Mango Publishing, established in 2014, publishes an eclectic list of books by diverse authors—both new and established voices—on topics ranging from business, personal growth, women's empowerment, LGBTQ studies, health, and spirituality to history, popular culture, time management, decluttering, lifestyle, mental wellness, aging, and sustainable living. We were recently named 2019's #1 fastest growing independent publisher by *Publishers Weekly*. Our success is driven by our main goal, which is to publish high quality books that will entertain readers as well as make a positive difference in their lives.

Our readers are our most important resource; we value your input, suggestions, and ideas. We'd love to hear from you—after all, we are publishing books for you!

Please stay in touch with us and follow us at:

Facebook: Mango Publishing
Twitter: @MangoPublishing
Instagram: @MangoPublishing
LinkedIn: Mango Publishing
Pinterest: Mango Publishing

Sign up for our newsletter at www.mangopublishinggroup.com and receive a free book!

Join us on Mango's journey to reinvent publishing, one book at a time.